WINNING

trotman

Winning CVs for First-time Job Hunters
This second edition published in 2004 by Trotman and Company Ltd
2 The Green, Richmond, Surrey TW9 1PL

Reprinted 2004
Reprinted 2005

Editorial and Publishing Team
Author Kathleen Houston
Editorial Mina Patria, Editorial Director; Rachel Lockhart, Commissioning Editor; Anya Wilson, Editor; Bianca Knights, Assistant Editor
Production Ken Ruskin, Head of Pre-press and Production
Sales and Marketing Deborah Jones, Head of Sales and Marketing
Advertising Tom Lee, Commercial Director
Managing Director Toby Trotman

Design by XAB

British Library Cataloguing in Publication Data
A catalogue record for this book is available from the British Library

ISBN 0 85660 971 4

Typeset by Mac Style Ltd, Scarborough, N. Yorkshire
Printed and bound in Great Britain by Bell & Bain Ltd, Glasgow, Scotland

contents

About the author

Kathleen Houston is a working careers adviser, a professional career coach and trainer. She has experience of advising university, college and school students, as well as mature career returners and those facing the challenge of redundancy. Most recently, she has shared her expertise on programmes for national and local radio stations. She is enthusiastic about helping people go for their dreams and has been successful in helping people do just that. She is also a web content writer and author of three other books, published by Trotman. With her own varied career portfolio, she believes that she is living her own dream!

First thoughts

'Let me do that for you!' Now think hard about that small phrase – it just might be the most pleasing phrase in the English language. When we hear it, we can almost feel the load shifting before we even say, 'Yes, I'll take you up on that offer!' There are about a hundred things in every day that we would be happy to dump on some willing person, from sitting in the dentist's chair to riding to school in the rain, to finishing that tricky homework or even completing that boring assignment! How many things in every day would you be happy to offload? It would be almost like having a stand-in for stuff that is boring, exhausting or just a waste of time.

Now here's the point – sometimes you can't just appear at the door of every prospective employer, to tell them how wonderful and perfect you are for that great work experience placement, part-time job, gap year job or whatever. You have to send or email your stand-in – your perfect in every detail, on top form CV (abbreviation for the rather cumbersome Latin phrase 'curriculum vitae' meaning the course of your life). You can let your stand-in do it all for you!

Just imagine if an employer came seeking you out today – you'd be unprepared, perhaps a little ragged around the edges, you might stammer a bit with nerves or just panic. What if you could just call on your stand-in – the perfectly packaged CV – spruced up and ready for action.

The best thing about a great CV is that it *is* you, shined up and slicked back, on your best day. Think of yourself as some small grubby boy who has been fishing on a summer's day and comes home for tea to be surprised by the unexpected arrival of some very important visitor. Grubby boy is a great character but is not looking or sounding his best, so nervy parents would wash him down, tidy him up, wet down his hair and present him as a perfect specimen. Well that's what you will have to do to yourself to create a great CV – take the whole magnificent sprawl of yourself and make it into a nice neat package.

This is what this book is about – if you've read this far, you're probably really hoping that someone will say, 'Let me do your CV for you' and that would be pretty terrific, but, and it's the usual big 'but', I can kind of promise that this book will break the job down, make it easy, but you'll still have to do some work yourself (perhaps open up the top of your head and do some deep and meaningful stuff) but of course it will be worth it.

Here are some quick reasons for doing it:

- It's easier than you think.
- Once you've done your first CV, you can kind of squidge it around and let it morph into more advanced CVs as you go along.
- It can be quite uplifting, when you sit down and realise just how unique and wonderful you are.
- If you do it right, you will feel pretty good about yourself.

So that's it really – an offer you can't refuse. But just a small warning: there are some ready-made, example CVs in this book and you might feel tempted to say, 'I'll have one of those' and skip to those sections. Be strong and work through the first few chapters so that you really know what you're about and what you need by way of a CV. It will be worth the time and effort!

1

Why a CV?
What's it for?

You may be a season ticket holder for your favourite football team. You may be a member of a fan club for your favourite band. You may have a student ID card that gets you discounts in clubs and shops. You may have a driving licence or even a credit card. All these things tell people about you: they get you in places, on the basis of what they say about you – they get you in or past something. A CV, apart from being a summary of your personal history to date, does just the same: it reassures an employer and says, 'Consider me – let me in!'

It is of course just the briefest representation of you (Americans call it a resumé). It's a bit like the menu in a restaurant: it tells an employer what to expect, it helps an employer know what to pick from. However, just as the menu is not the real food you will eat in a restaurant (you don't eat the menu, unless you are seriously weird) so your CV isn't you, just a representation of you. Now some CVs are impostors, pretending to be someone, but in fact they are either total fantasies (mostly lies) or just plain dull.

When they are fantasy based, they are a bit like a brilliant menu that doesn't live up to your expectations. You pick out something from the menu with a fancy name, but when the food arrives and you eat it, it tastes quite ordinary and is disappointing.

However, there is nothing that tricky about creating a real, living, breathing CV, as long as you are a real, living, breathing person to start with! It's just that sometimes, CV myths and well-meaning advice from friends, relatives and teachers can stop you from creating the brilliant CV you want. Let's take a look at a few CV myths!

CV MYTHS – DON'T BELIEVE THEM

1 You need to make things up on CVs, otherwise you won't sound good

2 You need lots of work history/experience to write a CV

3 You need great qualifications on a CV

4 A CV has to be at least 2 pages long

5 A CV has to be presented in a binder or a folder

6 The CV has to show every hour of your life

7 A CV has to have names, addresses and telephone numbers of at least three references

8 You have to have hobbies and interests to make yourself seem interesting

9 You have to make it sound formal and use impressive words

10 You don't need a CV for most jobs, and if you do, you can fish an old one out and send it off

All of these statement are false. Let me explain some of them.

1 Making things up

Making things up really won't work, but writing about yourself in a positive, confident way will. Employers who read CVs are not mind readers, so don't expect them to guess things that you assume they will know. You can *write yourself up*, rather than make things up. What this means is that you make it clear that work, study or life experience has given you something that may be of use to them.

For example, if you have only had one job as a milk delivery person, you may think it's too unimportant to mention, when in reality, the fact that you regularly and reliably got up at 4 am to deliver milk in all weathers is really quite impressive. Writing it up is offering the important detail beyond just the milk round job!

2   Little or no work experience
In terms of little or no work experience, that is quite immaterial unless you make it so. For example, if you have the heading 'Work Experience' on your CV and then put nothing in that section, that's a waste of space. You either have to insert something relevant in that section – perhaps some volunteer work, raising money in a sponsored run or helping out a relative for example – or just delete that section from your CV. Everyone has to get their first job and if you haven't ever had one, you will not have any experience yet! However, you can still write an interesting CV, and that's what you will learn as you go through this book.

3   Poor or zero qualifications
In the same way, qualifications do not make or break a CV – the sum total of who you are is about what you have done, what you are doing and what you plan to do – and that's what should be on your CV. If your qualifications are minimal or non-existent, you just need to make sure that other sections on the CV make up for this.

4   How long should a CV be?
There is no set length for a CV, although long (over two pages) CVs are not recommended. Remember that employers are busy and so a CV that tells them just enough to get them interested is ideal. A typical school leaver's CV is likely to be just a page long.

5   Flash binders or folders?
Binders or folders on CVs are pretty but unnecessary and can be quite costly if you are sending out a lot of CVs. Stick to a simple document that is well presented and has interesting language and content – that will be impressive enough.

6   A diary of your life to date?
As mentioned before, your CV is a representation of you, so it doesn't have to have every single hour of your life, just the key points that will be relevant to someone who might employ you. That rather interesting certificate you got at nursery school for being the best painter or playdoher can be left off your CV!

7 Do you need references?

It's quite useful to have a couple of people who can say good things about you and are willing, if required, to write a reference (a brief statement about your personal qualities or your employability – what you are like in a work situation), but you don't need to get hung up on this one. Think of asking a friend of the family and perhaps a favourite teacher or an employer if you have worked somewhere – ask them if they would be willing to offer you a reference, if you need one, *and ask their permission* to give their contact details to a future employer.

It's quite common to just have a line saying, 'References available on request' on your CV and as long as you have a couple of referees ready and willing, you can then send the names and addresses of referees at a later stage, when an employer has requested them. You can do this as an addendum page to your CV: this is an extra page you have ready, neatly wordprocessed with the two referees with names, addresses and telephone numbers detailed. This is far easier than putting these details on your original CV – it means you have more space for the really interesting things you want to say.

8 Hobbies and interests – why these might be useful

There are sections on hobbies/interests on many CVs, often in a final 'Personal' section; the only reason for giving these is if they say something special or unique about you. They can be valuable, because they give a sense of the real person behind the CV and can let an employer guess the kind of person you might be. However, don't manufacture hobbies or interests to make yourself seem sparkling!

Occasionally, an interest may actually work against you or give the wrong impression. Personally, I would think twice about having trainspotting as a hobby on a CV, not because I have anything against trainspotting, but because people as a rule make adverse judgements about trainspotting and trainspotters. On the other hand, if you were applying for a job with Virgin Trains, and you were a trainspotter, trainspotting might be exceedingly relevant!

Similarly, your support of a football team might cause a negative reaction in an employer who might support a rival team, so think about this one!

9 CV language

Two big errors on CVs are peculiarly formal, often dull language and the use of jargon words. A CV should be something that is easy to read and therefore your choice of words is important. That doesn't mean that it is OK to use abbreviated or slang language, but it does mean that simple, precise, natural language generally has more impact. Don't feel you have to take out a thesaurus to write a CV. Don't use jargon that might be meaningless to the reader.

10 Any old CV will do?
Finally, a CV has to be current – think of it as having a 'sell by' date. That means that you update it, change it, amend it, refresh it regularly, probably at least three or four times a year. Never send an old CV off – it would be like sending a mouldy piece of cheese to someone.

Who should you listen to about creating a compelling CV?

Well, I count myself as something of a CV guru, but I could just be another well-meaning fool, so I will tell you:

- Trust yourself and your own instincts.
- Listen to what employers say they want (ask them or read up about employers you would want to work for).

Now, I am going to make it easy for you by letting you in on what employers say they want on CVs – various people have asked employers up and down the country and throughout the world what they expect on CVs, and it turns out to be just a few key things, that make a lot of sense.

Be an employer for a moment

I wonder if you can guess what employers really want from a CV. Perhaps you could pretend to be an employer and guess what they might say. Imagine yourself sitting behind a desk. You're pretty tired and you have a pile of CVs to get through before you can go home – what would you want to see or hear about?

Take a moment to make some educated guesses and then check this next section to see if you are right.

What employers say they want from a CV

- Basic contact details – your name, address, telephone number (home and mobile) and email address, placed at the top of the CV, probably centred on the page, something like this:

Jack Cameron
5 Sussex Gardens
Hessington, Oxon OX1 1ZZ
Tel: 06677 8888 (home) 0998877 77 (mobile)
Email: jackin@email.org.uk

- Clear sections with headings like Education, Work Experience or Career History, Voluntary Work, Achievements, Key Skills, etc.
- A good logical sequence from section to section, which shows exactly what you have to offer in the most positive light.
- A good wordprocessed format that presents the information clearly.
- A section that describes your skills and achievements.
- A brief profile at the beginning that describes you, your career aims and what you are offering.
- An interesting personal section that gives a feel for the 'real you'.
- Lots of white space between sections so that it looks easy to read.
- A good clear font like Arial (some fonts look a bit fiddly – avoid Times New Roman for this reason).
- Clear language with absolutely zero spelling or punctuation errors.

So if you want to take anyone's advice, take it from the people who will read your CV – the employers or recruiters.

This is what we have done. Here are some possible actual or fictional comments, some of which are true and some less true – can you guess which seem to be the most likely comments that an employer might make?

True/False – what employers say about CVs quiz

EMPLOYER COMMENTS – TRUE OR FALSE?

1 Some CVs arrive on my desk and I have no idea why they have been sent to me

2 I like a one-page CV that just gives me the facts

3 I don't like unsolicited CVs – I just bin them

4 I'm generally impressed if someone has addressed the CV for my attention

5 Some CVs seem quite childlike in their simplicity

6 I want to be able to scan-read a CV in a few minutes

7 I like a CV which is well presented

8 I like a CV which has a photo of the applicant

9 I always reply to CVs

10 I often keep good CVs on file and get back to applicants when I have a vacancy

11 I like it when someone follows up a CV with a phone call

THE MOSTLY TRUES

Some CVs arrive on my desk and I have no idea why they have been sent to me

I have talked to employers who have actively turned against applicants who sent in a CV (in an envelope or via email) without explanation or forethought.

Employers reason that, even as a basic courtesy or encouragement to read the CV, a letter attached to it is needed (see Chapter 10, Covering letters). A lone CV is a little naked and embarrassed – a covering letter dresses up a CV and makes it look professional. In your covering letter you can explain why you are approaching that employer and what especially you can offer them.

I'm generally impressed if someone has addressed the CV for my attention

Employers are human beings and respond to courtesy. When you address them by name in the covering letter and on the outside of the envelope, it shows you have done your research. It also means that it is likely to get to the right person.

I like a CV which is well presented

This generally means that the CV is easy to read, logical and well word processed. It encourages the reader to read it because it is clear and has white spaces between sections and headings, which break up the text. If you choose to put the CV on coloured or even cream paper, it shows attention to detail and individuality.

I often keep good CVs on file and get back to applicants when I have a vacancy

As a general rule, small and medium-sized employers (SMEs) are more likely to do this. These SMEs offer about 90 per cent of the jobs that will be out there for you and often employ between one and 250 staff. They may not have a personnel or human resources department to deal with CVs and they may be glad to receive CVs that applicants send 'on the off chance'.

Talking to these employers, I found that they do in fact keep CVs on file in case a vacancy comes up. It saves them money to contact people who have sent them speculative CVs rather than pay for an expensive job advert.

I like it when someone follows up a CV with a phone call

In this case, particularly smaller or medium-sized employers claim to like being contacted by applicants who have sent them a speculative CV. Again, it might save them time or give them the chance to chat to you informally. In some ways, it is hardly worth sending a CV out into the blue and not following it up. Any conversations you have with an employer could later lead to a job offer.

THE LESS TRUE OR FALSE COMMENTS

I like a one-page CV that just gives me the facts

Most employers expect a two-page CV, but some like the idea of a one-page CV (sometimes called a résumé) because it takes less time to read and is less likely to have fluffy or useless information. Mostly you need to concentrate on creating something that someone will want to read – if you can do that in one page that is good; if it takes two pages, that will be fine.

I don't like unsolicited CVs – I just bin them

This is true for some employers – they may view an unrequested CV like a junk-mail letter. Many large employers state specifically that they only want you to send them a CV for a specific advertised job – if they say this, then take note of it. Nonetheless, there is always the chance that an unsolicited CV that lands on the right desk will strike a chord with someone, so do your research and if you can send a CV to a named person who has the power to recruit you, it may be worth it.

Some CVs seem quite childlike in their simplicity

There are some CVs that employers receive which puzzle them because they seem like something a primary school child might write. In addition, many covering letters are written in the same way they might have taught you to write letters at primary school. Typically, you may choose to send an old CV, which you did for your Record of Achievement or Progress File in Year 9 – this probably does you no favours a few years later. So the best advice is to realise that a CV needs to be a living, breathing thing and not a document that is part of your early childhood memories. It needs to be updated, revised, refreshed and sometimes re-created from scratch.

I want to be able to scan-read a CV in a few minutes

Time is always short for employers and for some a quick scan-read is best. However, when deciding on who should be selected for interview, employers generally read CVs with some attention to detail, which can take longer than a few minutes.

I like a CV which has a photo of the applicant

Most UK employers do not like photos with CVs. It is sometimes more common on American CVs or for jobs where your appearance might be vital, such as acting or modelling.

I always reply to CVs

I wish this one were true, but unfortunately, the norm is that most employers do not respond to CVs, particularly if they are speculative. Some, in job adverts, state:

'If you have not heard from us within two weeks of the application deadline, you can assume that you have not been selected on this occasion.'

So, if you do receive a reply, even a rejection letter, you can count yourself lucky in some ways. This means that it is a good idea to keep a detailed record of CVs sent which you can then follow up by phone, in the event of a lack of response.

CV Don'ts

While we're on the subject of what employers want, here are a few things to avoid – these are quotes from real-life employers.

'I get bored with seeing the same old CV format all the time – there seem to be some recommended on the Internet – the CV wizards – which are frankly a bit old hat.'

'The name, address, date of birth CV with the barest information does nothing for me – it looks like a skeleton that needs fleshing out!'

'If I come across a misspelling in a CV, I stop reading – why should I bother, if an applicant can't be bothered!'

'There is a line between being overmodest and arrogant. Most applicants go for one or the other. Overmodest isn't honest – I want them to tell me what they can do well. Arrogant is dishonest – I don't expect applicants to be good at everything, but I want to know what they are good at.'

CVtip
Don't waffle

CV QUIZ TO CLEAR YOUR MIND

Here's a simple quiz that will get you thinking in the right way and will act as the perfect preparation for your own CV writing.

1   A CV – what's it really for?

a) To tell an employer about yourself

b) To list your education and work experience

c) To persuade an employer to offer you an interview

2   How much time does the average recruiter take to read a CV?

a) 10 minutes

b) 5 minutes

c) 30 seconds

3   How many pages long should a CV be?

a) 1 page

b) 2 pages

c) 30 seconds

4   What colour paper should you use?

a) White

b) Cream

c) Some bright colour

5   What is the smallest font size you can use for the text in your CV?

a) 12

b) 10

c) 8

6   How should you keep the pages of your CV together?

a) A staple

b) A paper clip

c) Nothing – leave them loose

7   Should a good CV have a personal profile section?

a) Yes

b) No

8 Do you need a different CV for each job you apply for?

a) Yes

b) No

9 About how many lines of text should you aim for in each section or paragraph?

a) 10 lines

b) 5 lines

c) 3 lines

10 How will you check your CV for errors or for 'good flow'?

a) Show it to a friend

b) Show it to a teacher

c) Show it to an employer

d) Show it to two or three people

- -

1 A CV – what's it really for?

c) To persuade an employer to offer you an interview

There are a lot of reasons for sending a CV, but the bottom line is that you want the employer to be desperate to meet you! So, the key aim is to tempt them to offer you an interview or to ask you in for an informal chat. If you have just sent your CV to an employer on the off-chance or speculatively, then the offer of an informal chat is a good result.

2 How much time does the average recruiter take to read a CV?

c) 30 seconds

Some take longer, some take less time, but 30 seconds is the average, so it means that your CV has to stand out from the pile and the language has to reach out and grab them.

3 How many pages long should a CV be?

b) 2 pages

Two pages is a good maximum – if you can't do it in two pages, then you are waffling. There are some wordprocessing tricks to help you get a lot on each page, which are covered in Chapter 3.

4 **What colour paper should you use?**

a), b) and c)

This is an interesting one. Most CVs are on white, good quality paper (not just average printer paper – go to a stationers and get a decent paper with a little weight to it, so your CV prints out well onto it) and white is fine for most CVs. However, cream can look very professional and a little different.

You may choose to go for bright coloured paper, but consider this carefully – it might work for certain razzmatazz employers, such as the media or advertising, but may not go down well with a legal firm. So the answer is, stick to cream or white for traditional employers or if you are not sure what they are like, and go for coloured paper to make a bold statement, if it fits the employer.

5 **What is the smallest font size you can use for the text in your CV?**

b) 10

Most CVs are created in a font size of between 10 and 12. I find size 11 works well for headings with 10 for the main text.

6 **How should you keep the pages of your CV together?**

a) A staple

Most CVs have the two pages stapled together in the corner. If they are loose or paper clipped, they need to be well identified with your name and details on each page, in case the two pages get separated, so stapling is simpler and safer. Binders may look good, but the postage will cost more and if an employer wants to photocopy your CV to send it elsewhere, it can be a nuisance.

7 **Should a good CV have a personal profile section?**

a) Yes

Most good CVs have a personal profile section of some kind, either at the beginning or end of the CV, or sometimes at the beginning *and* end of the CV – see the various examples in this book. The idea is that if an employer scan-reads a CV, they may read the beginning and then flick to the end, so the beginning and end should have something really interesting.

8   **Do you need a different CV for each job you apply for?**

a) Yes

There is no such thing as a multi-purpose CV, but you can have a good template CV saved on your computer, which may be the fullest version of who you are, what you can do, etc. Every time you want to apply for a job, you can call up your template and tweak and edit it so that it fits the job you are applying for. You may emphasise certain skills and delete other bits that seem less relevant. Customising your CV to each employer or job is a guarantee of a warm welcome for your CV. You will be able to save each customised version of your template, so you may end up with several versions of your CV.

9   **About how many lines of text should you aim for in each section or paragraph?**

b) 5 lines

Around five lines of text is about right with a line space or section heading before the next block of lines. This makes it easy to read and chunks the information down for the reader.

10 **How will you check your CV for errors or for 'good flow'?**

d) Show it to two or three people

It is a good idea to find two or three CV critics that you trust, perhaps a friend who is working, a friend of the family who works in a Human Resources or Personnel department, an English teacher or a careers adviser or teacher. Consider all their criticisms, correct any errors and then decide for yourself if it works as a document to represent you! Remember this is your stand-in – a famous actor wouldn't employ a stand-in who didn't faithfully represent him by the way he looked and in the action sequences. Your CV has to look real and sound really like you – be sure that it does!

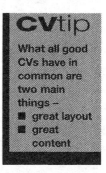

CVtip

What all good CVs have in common are two main things –
■ great layout
■ great content

So now that we've got some of the basics out of the way and pummelled you into submission with some CV myths and the CV quiz, we can take a look at how you create a whizz bang CV that will get you noticed.

chapter

2

The how of CVs

Knowing how to create a CV that works to get you that part-time job, that work experience placement, that first job after leaving school or college or even that gap year job is just a question of choosing and selecting carefully – a kind of glorified pick and mix exercise. If you go to the cinema regularly, you might have seen those pick and mix bars – you have a few moments before the film starts and you have to make decisions on the best mixture to take in with you. You have to weigh things up and then the assistant weighs it up for you to tell you the price. Your weighing up may be about whether jelly babies will make you thirsty, or whether rainbow choc buttons will make you sticky.

Well, creating a CV that will get you the job is pretty much the same – there's a whole lot of things to pick from and you have to weigh it all up and decide. They have to jostle along together in the CV bag, so they have to be the right mix. Here are the typical pick and mix ingredients that appear on most CVs, but remember, you don't have to pick every one – it's up to you to choose what makes sense to you. Nonetheless, the basic contacts section at the beginning is pretty vital, as without that you will be a brilliant Mr/Ms Nobody.

Contact details
Name, Address, Telephone number, Email, etc.

Career aim/Personal profile/
Self-marketing statement

Example – A confident, reliable school leaver with retail experience, seeking customer service work.

Key skills/Experience/Achievements
Example –
- Communication skills, developed through English coursework and vacation hospitality event work at busy racecourse
- Proven reliability, shown by part-time paper round over two years
- Young Enterprise award winner

Education history/Education and qualifications
Example –
2002–04 **Bladon College**
3 A-levels in English, Textiles and History achieved

Work experience/Career history
Example –
2002–2004 Fried Chicken Company
Catering assistant, promoted to supervisor after 6 months

Training courses
2002 Food Hygiene certificate passed
2003 First Aid qualification achieved through Red Cross

Volunteer experience
Example – Last summer in my vacation I worked on a local play scheme for learning-disabled children, offering sporting and craft activities to children aged 7 to 15 years. As well as being tremendous fun, this helped me realise that a career in social work or care would really suit me.

Personal
Example – I am a quietly confident person and in a work situation I can be flexible and work on my own initiative. In a recent part-time job at a fast food restaurant, I had to think on my feet when a small child seemed to be choking. By supporting the parents and staying calm, I was able to prevent a serious problem from developing. In my spare time, I enjoy shopping, reading and spending time with friends.

References
Example – Either names and addresses of two referees, one person who knows you personally (not a family member) and one who knows you from school, college or work, or just state, 'Excellent references available on request.'

How to assemble your CV

Take a look at all the headings in the figure above – these are the most common sections on a CV, but you may not need them all. You have to decide on the most appropriate sections for your purposes, to reflect your uniqueness. Here is an example of a very simple school leaver CV, and the same CV with a slightly different mix and sequence, which will give each CV a slightly different emphasis.

JACK CAMERON

5 Sussex Gardens, Hessington, Oxon OX1 1ZZ
Tel: 099987 66544
Email: jacking@email.org.uk

I am a hardworking, reliable Year 10 pupil, with a strong interest in sport and coaching, keen to gain work experience in a gym or fitness centre.

KEY ACHIEVEMENTS

- Competed at regional sportsday, representing school and county at 100m
- Captain of school football and tennis teams
- 100% attendance record at school for 4 years

EDUCATION

1999 – present   Hessington High School
Currently studying for ten GCSEs in English, Maths, History, Biology, Design Technology, French, Business Studies, PE, Drama and RE. Predicted grades for final exams – As and Bs.

WORK EXPERIENCE

2002 – present   Hessington Golf Driving Range
Part-time work three times a week dealing with golf customers, selling golfing goods and collecting golf balls.

2000 – 2002   Hessington News
Paper delivery person, starting at 6am, five mornings a week.

PERSONAL

I am an active, outdoor person and have played sport at school and club level. My favourite sports are football, tennis and golf. My career aims are to either play sport at a professional level or to work in the sports industry. My part-time work has helped develop my confidence and customer service skills.

REFERENCES

I can provide references on request.

Now the basic information on this CV can be picked and mixed in a different way, depending on what the person is applying for. Two years later, when Jack wanted to work with kids on an American camp, his CV was tweaked to look like this.

College student CV

JACK CAMERON

5 Sussex Gardens, Hessington, Oxon OX1 1ZZ
Tel: 09998 766544
Email: jacking@email.org.uk

An A-level student with voluntary playscheme experience with 4 to 15 year olds and a strong interest in sport, seeking summer camp work abroad.

KEY ACHIEVEMENTS AND SKILLS

* Leadership skills through voluntary playscheme work and being captain of school and college teams
* Teamwork skills through sporting achievements and part-time work
* First Aid skills, proven by recent certificates
* Employee of the month at Dynamo Sports for excellent customer service.

EMPLOYMENT EXPERIENCE

2003 – present   **Dynamo Sports**
Saturday and evening part-time work, alongside A-level study, demonstrating sports equipment in a major sports retailer.

2002 – 2003   **Hessington Golf Driving Range**
Part-time work three times a week dealing with golf customers, selling golfing goods and collecting golf balls.

2000 – 2002   **Hessington News**
Paper delivery person, starting at 6am, five mornings a week.

EDUCATION

2003 – present   **Hessington College**
Currently studying A-levels in PE, English and Psychology – predicted grades three Bs.

1999 – 2000   **Hessington High School**
Achieved ten GCSEs in English (A), Maths (B), History (B), Biology (C), Design Technology (C), French (B), Business Studies (C), PE (A), Drama (A) and RE (B).

VOLUNTEER EXPERIENCE

Last summer in my vacation I worked on a local play scheme for learning-disabled children, offering sporting and craft activities to children aged 7 to 15 years. As well as being tremendous fun, this helped me realise that I relate well to children and can cope with large groups of children with humour and confidence.

PERSONAL

I am an active, outdoor person and have played sport at school and club level. My favourite sports are football, tennis and golf. My career aims are either to play sport at a professional level or to work in the sports industry, preferably in a coaching capacity. My part-time work has helped develop my confidence, my customer service skills and an ability to think on my feet. In my spare time, I enjoy most sports and have recently taken up water skiing.

REFERENCES
I can provide references on request.

As you can see, there are just a few changes to show how Jack has grown and developed, but in essence it is the same CV. You'll notice that the sequence of the sections has been changed to place more importance on his employment experience and his volunteering.

So what everyone needs is a template or starting-point CV that has their basic information and history, which can then be amended or moved around for particular job applications or as time goes on.

CV in a nutshell

Before we move on to the 'How to' of creating a template CV, it's worth realising that a nutshell CV is just the essence of a full CV, the absolute minimum that every employer is looking for. Think of that weary employer again, with a pile of CVs on his or her desk. What are the three key things he or she wants to know about you? They probably break down into the following:

- your personality qualities
- your skills (what you can do with evidence to prove this)
- your experience of work or, if you have little of this, any transferable skills from study or life experience.

PERSONALITY

Yes, you have one! There is something unique about you; how would you describe yourself? Ask around – your friends and family will come up with good words to describe you (ignore the negatives). Are you happy, confident, quiet, reliable, resourceful, hardworking, funny, sociable, honest? Using a thesaurus, look up alternatives for the words people use about you. Even the negative ones can have a positive spin: for example, 'stubborn' could be transformed into 'determined'! Make a list of strong, scintillating adjectives that really fit you and that you could prove, if required. If you need help with this, have a look through the 'CV Power Words' at the end of this chapter.

SKILLS

Skills confuse people a bit, but here are the most common skills that many of us possess – check which ones you could lay claim to:

- Communication skills – being able to talk, listen and present information.
- Interpersonal skills – being able to relate to other people, mix well, being interested in people.
- Numerical skills – being confident with numbers, basic arithmetic, maths, etc.
- Analytical skills – being able to analyse information and make sense of it.
- Problem-solving skills – being able to offer solutions to problems, being able to work through things.
- Teamwork skills – the ability to work with others to achieve something.
- Leadership skills – being willing to take responsibility, and encourage others.
- Information technology skills – the ability to use computers at basic or advanced levels.
- Initiative skills – the ability to work on your own without constant supervision.
- Organisational skills – the ability to organise your time and work to deadlines.

Now it may be that you have all these skills, but most of us have particular skills that are stronger – you need to select your best ones and remember, you will be asked for evidence or proof that you have these skills so be ready with a 'for example'. If you state that you can offer teamwork skills, your example might be, 'I have worked 12-hour days as part of a catering team at the Golf Open.'

YOUR EXPERIENCE OR TRANSFERABLE SKILLS

Just about the smallest work experience is valuable in proving that you are *employable*: that's what employers really want, so don't forget anything that could be useful.

You might have helped out at a school fete, organised a charity fun run, worked for a day to help a friend of the family or put up some posters for a craft fair. Even with little experience, there are some things you've done that suggest that you could do something else. If you did help out at a school fete, you could claim organisational skills; if you didn't, then surely organising your revision timetable for GCSE exams with coursework deadlines is an alternative way of proving organisational skills.

There's always a way of proving transferable skills, if you really do some thinking about the whole of your life and the things you do. 'Transferable' just means that something you do in one part of your life could be deemed useful for work purposes. So if you have been a scorer for your local cricket team, you could offer proof of being reliable and honest, as well as being able to take criticism. This skill or experience could be usefully transferred and used as evidence that you are a suitable applicant for a job in a shop, when on occasion you might have to deal with difficult customers.

CV nutshelling

This is how it goes: for interview preparation and CV preparation, you need a minimal amount of information, so if you can write two or three sentences in the three categories above you have your CV in a nutshell, which is a great starting point. So start collecting information about the following:

- your three strongest and best personality qualities
- your strongest and best skills, with examples to prove them
- your experience in any work environment or your key transferable skills.

Now you have got the basis of a really compelling CV. Next, take a moment to look through your Record of Achievement, Progress File or your certificates and make a list of dates of when you started secondary school, sixth form or college, any part-time jobs, work experience, etc and actual dates of passing exams. If you've done all that, you're ready to start building your template CV.

Template CV building – the easy way

Decide which sections you will need for your CV – you will probably have the usual ones but may want to add or remove any sections according to your life experiences. It helps to do the next bit on a computer – type the following section headings into a basic Word document:

- Contact Details
- Beginning Profile statement or Career Aim
- Education History or Education and Qualifications
- Work Experience or Career or Employment History
- Voluntary Work (optional)
- Personal section
- References

Set up the document below in Arial and then start filling in your details in the sections as follows. Here's an example of what this bare-bones CV template might look like:

NAME

Address
Telephone number
Email

PERSONAL PROFILE

KEY SKILLS AND ACHIEVEMENTS

EDUCATION AND QUALIFICATIONS

Date   **School/College**

WORK EXPERIENCE OR EMPLOYMENT HISTORY

Date   **Employer**

VOLUNTARY WORK

PERSONAL

REFERENCES

Assembling your template CV

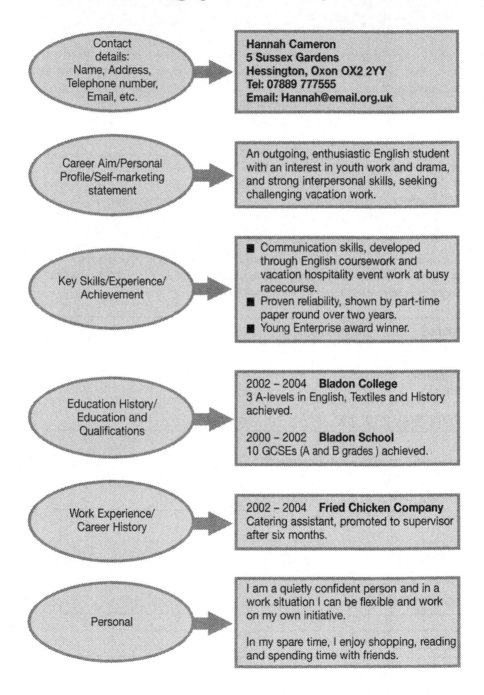

Contact details: Name, Address, Telephone number, Email, etc.

> Hannah Cameron
> 5 Sussex Gardens
> Hessington, Oxon OX2 2YY
> Tel: 07889 777555
> Email: Hannah@email.org.uk

Career Aim/Personal Profile/Self-marketing statement

> An outgoing, enthusiastic English student with an interest in youth work and drama, and strong interpersonal skills, seeking challenging vacation work.

Key Skills/Experience/ Achievement

> - Communication skills, developed through English coursework and vacation hospitality event work at busy racecourse.
> - Proven reliability, shown by part-time paper round over two years.
> - Young Enterprise award winner.

Education History/ Education and Qualifications

> 2002 – 2004   **Bladon College**
> 3 A-levels in English, Textiles and History achieved.
>
> 2000 – 2002   **Bladon School**
> 10 GCSEs (A and B grades) achieved.

Work Experience/ Career History

> 2002 – 2004   **Fried Chicken Company**
> Catering assistant, promoted to supervisor after six months.

Personal

> I am a quietly confident person and in a work situation I can be flexible and work on my own initiative.
>
> In my spare time, I enjoy shopping, reading and spending time with friends.

Draft format CV – how it comes together

HANNAH CAMERON

---

5 Sussex Gardens, Hessington, Oxon OX2 2YY
Tel: 07889 777555
Email: hannah@email.org.uk

An outgoing, enthusiastic English student with an interest in youth work and drama and strong interpersonal skills, seeking challenging vacation work.

KEY SKILLS AND ACHIEVEMENTS

Communication skills, developed through English coursework and vacation hospitality event work at busy racecourse.

Proven reliability, shown by part-time paper round over two years.

Youth Enterprise award winner.

EDUCATION AND QUALIFICATIONS

2002 – 2004   **Bladon College**
3 A-levels in English, Textiles and History achieved.

2000 – 2002   **Bladon School**
10 GCSEs (A and B grades) achieved.

WORK EXPERIENCE

2002 – 2004   **Fried Chicken Company**
Catering assistant, promoted to supervisor after six months.

PERSONAL

I am a quietly confident person and in a work situation I can be flexible and work on my own initiative.

In my spare time I enjoy shopping, reading and spending time with friends.

Just add the reference section and the CV is virtually there in a draft format. This is just to show you how picking and mixing sections and filling them in can create a unique template CV which you can then customise according to the jobs you are going for.

The tricky sections

CVtip

White space on a CV is crucial – this is the space between sections that breaks the CV up into manageable chunks for the reader.

Most people find the basic information sections easy, but find it tough to create the beginning Personal Profile statement, the Key Skills section and the final Personal section, so here are a few pointers.

The beginning Personal Profile statement

This has to show your best personal qualities, skills and probably your future career aim or what you are looking for at that moment. Here are some examples:

'A caring, honest Health and Social Care student with strong communication and organisational skills, planning to train for nursing or midwifery.'

(This is a career objective or career aim profile statement.)

'A practical, reliable vehicle mechanic with strong technical skills, seeking a career change into automotive design.'

(This is a profile explaining a new career direction.)

'An outgoing, innovative advertising student with strong copywriting skills and a passion for fashion.'

(This is just a self-marketing statement type of profile – a kind of statement of fact, designed to excite interest in the applicant.)

Here is a foolproof mini template for writing the Personal Profile bit:

'A ... (first personality quality adjective), ... (second similar adjective) ... (describe your current situation, eg student, job title) with strong or excellent ... (describe best skill) skills, seeking ... (state work you are looking for or eventual career aim).'

Here's another example:

'An enthusiastic, sporty A-level student with coaching skills and qualifications and experience of managing a local football team, seeking interesting work opportunities.'

Key Skills/Achievements section

Aim for three or four bullet points with your best skills or achievements and give evidence of them at the same time. When you say you have great organisational skills, show how and why – for example:

'Organisational skills, developed through university coursework and through part-time work at a call centre.'

Final Personal section

Aim for about two short paragraphs. One should start, 'I am ...' and give a brief description of you and your personal motivation, for example:

'I am an energetic, enthusiastic person and in a work situation I like to set myself high standards and get the job done well. My present career aim is to train for public relations after degree study, so I welcome the chance to work in a marketing department.'

The second paragraph can start with, 'In my spare time ...' and you can mention any hobbies or interests.

So that's the basic template CV. For customising it further, we explore your CV's true mission in Chapter 3, but before we go there, here is that list of CV Power Words that might just inspire you or add extra flavour to your CV:

CVtip

When you meet someone for the first time, you pick up clues from them from: the way they look; the way they sound; subtle things that their body language conveys.

In the same way, an employer picks up clues about you from your CV from: the way your CV looks (the trouble you have taken); the way your CV sounds (the words and phrases you use); subtle things that come through, that they make guesses about, from what you say.

CV Power Words

Accurate	Confident	Flexible	Perceptive
Adaptable	Consistent	Friendly	Proficient
Analytical	Creative	Hard-working	Reliable
Articulate	Dedicated	Honest	Resourceful
Bilingual-	Dependable	Imaginative	Skilled
Business-minded	Dynamic	Innovative	Successful
Calm	Efficient	Keen	Tenacious
Capable	Energetic	Logical	Thorough
Commercially minded	Enthusiastic	Methodical	Trustworthy
Committed	Experienced	Motivated	Versatile
Competent	Expert	Organised	Willing

3

Your mission, should you choose to accept it ...

Well, it's not 'Mission Impossible', but nonetheless your CV has to have a purpose, a mission, and this clear purpose will affect the way your CV looks and sounds. There are actually many different styles and formats of CVs, according to what they are, ultimately, trying to achieve.

The mission, in a silly espionage sense, really does control how a spy acts. He or she might prepare for the mission through research and get into role beforehand. Your CV preparation and drafting are important, but what you do with that draft and how you customise and tweak it will be based on what you want the CV to actually do – the outcome you are looking for. Here are some possible missions that you might plan for your CV at different stages of your life:

- I need a CV to get a Saturday job in a garden centre – speculative/targeted.
- I need a CV to send to my possible work experience employer – requested/targeted.
- I've seen a job advertised that seems interesting and they want me to send my CV – requested/targeted.
- I need a CV to take with me to my university interview – requested/targeted.
- I want to persuade a local radio station to let me work-shadow a DJ, to see if that work would suit me – speculative/targeted.
- I want to send lots of CVs round to various local garages to see about getting a bodyshop apprenticeship – speculative/targeted.
- I want to move from my job in a factory into an office job – career progression/speculative/targeted.
- I'm leaving school soon and want to send a CV to various local employers – speculative/targeted.
- There are some jobs going where my uncle works and he says he will take my CV in to the human resources department – requested and speculative/targeted.
- I want a good job with training after my A-levels with a major bank and they have said that I can attach my CV to their application form – requested/targeted.
- I am taking a break before I go to university and want two or three different CVs to send off, to get different kinds of gap year experience – speculative/targeted.
- I'm at university and desperately need a part-time job to fit around my studies – speculative/targeted.

Let's look at these in a bit more detail.

Speculative/targeted CVs

It may be that you are vaguely interested in some kind of horticulture as a future career. You might think that a Saturday job in a garden centre would be a smart way of finding out more. It certainly would be! Alternatively, you might just fancy a garden centre because it would be quite an active job and offer variety.

Any Saturday job is going to give you the chance to develop skills and experience and earn a little money. So what kind of purpose does your CV need to show?

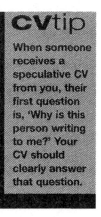

Well, it is likely that you would need a *speculative* CV for this purpose. 'Speculative' just means that you would send a good CV 'on the off chance' to various employers. It would state clearly what you are interested in and why. For speculative CVs to work, you need to do your research and 'target' your CV to the kind of employers likely to offer the kind of work that you want. Here's a short example of someone who sent a *speculative, targeted* CV on a mission!

CVtip

When someone receives a speculative CV from you, their first question is, 'Why is this person writing to me?' Your CV should clearly answer that question.

Sarah and her Saturday job

Sarah is a really creative, artistic 16-year-old and wanted to earn some extra money by taking on a Saturday job. She is hoping to do something vaguely artistic in the future and currently loves sewing, designing and making things. She didn't want to travel too far to work, so she did some reconnaissance in her local area, and found two or three shops that were interesting. One was a hobbies and crafts shop, one was a patchwork shop and another was a cake decorating shop. She went into each of these shops and checked she liked the way they dealt with customers and what the atmosphere was like in each place.

She wondered whether she should just walk in one day and ask about jobs, but although she is quite confident, she thought that might be a little scary! She decided to write a CV and target those particular employers. She thought she could phone them a week after sending the CV to see what they could offer her.

Now this is where she really was clever – she needed a *speculative and targeted CV*. She decided to assemble the basic information about herself in the three sections and it looked like this:

SARAH COTTON

10 Winchilsea Road, Cottonwood, Berks BB1 2YT
Tel: 09876 654545
Email: sc@email.org.uk

2001 – present   Cottonwood High
Currently studying 10 GCSEs including English, Maths, Textiles and Art

INTERESTS

Swimming, drawing, watercolour painting.

It didn't look like much! Next she decided to flesh it out a bit by adding three extra sections – a self-marketing statement, explaining what she was seeking, a section covering her best skills, and a personal section showing her current career motivation. This is how it shaped up:

SARAH COTTON

10 Winchilsea Road, Cottonwood, Berks BB1 2YT
Tel: 09876 654545
Email: sc@email.org.uk

I am a self-motivated, energetic person with a real interest in arts and crafts and creative/artistic skills, seeking a Saturday job where I can use my interests and offer excellent customer service in a retail environment.

KEY SKILLS
- I love to sew, design and make things, and last year I won a school prize for designing a wall hanging.
- I help run a Brownie pack and as a Guider I have to be confident and enthusiastic talking to children and their parents.
- I am, I think, quite unusually organised and tidy – I like to know where things are and what I am supposed to be doing.

EDUCATION HISTORY – SO FAR

2001 – present   Cottonwood High
Currently studying 10 GCSEs including English, Maths, Textiles and Art.
I tend to get highest grades in the subjects that I enjoy, but I am aiming to gain at least pass grades in my less than favourite subjects and A grades in Textiles and Art.

VOLUNTARY WORK

Once a week, I help run a Brownie pack which involves play, art and craft and sporting activities with 7–11-year-olds. It's great fun and hard work.

PERSONAL

Other than that I enjoy swimming for a competitive team, drawing and watercolour painting. My gran decorates cakes, so I have been able to learn some basic water paste and decorating skills.

REFERENCES

My form tutor and my Guide leader are happy to offer references for my reliability for a Saturday job.

Please see next page for samples of my creative work.

What Sarah attached to her one-page, rather exceptional CV, was a page where she had scanned in photos of some of her creative work – this really gave her potential employers proof of what she was capable of. Let me tell you what happened next. Sarah sent three CVs off to her targeted employers. She planned to wait a week and then phone them. A day after sending her CVs, she received three phone calls asking if she would come for interviews. She got offered the first job she went for in the patchwork shop!

So that, I hope, has made a really good case for sending speculative CVs, but in most cases, they need to be targeted if they are to have a good chance of hitting the right spot.

CVtip

Being modest and unassuming on a CV is the worst and most common mistake!

Remember that employers are not mindreaders – unless you tell them what you can do for them they simply won't know.

Scatter gun or sureshooter

Many people make the mistake of sending out 100 CVs in rather a random fashion to just anyone, anywhere, hoping it will work. It rarely does!

Scattergunning CVs into the blue hardly ever hits the right mark, while sureshooting with your eye on your targets is far more likely to be met with success.

So whenever you need to send a CV which is intended to generate a possible job offer, whether it be for part-time work, to gain experience or for your first job, you will need a compelling and interesting CV that is customised to the kind of employers you are interested in (in other words, it suits that employer) and very clearly outlines what you are hoping for and what you can offer.

Requested/targeted CVs

There will be many times that you are asked to send a CV or where a job advert requires one, and although this may seem easier, it demands just as careful attention and targeting. The employer will have given you some clues in their advert or application pack and will be expecting you to show how you match the requirements of the job. Let's take a look at a typical job advert that might attract a first year university student, needing some part-time work.

> **Dynamic, motivated Call Centre staff required for mail order catalogue company.**
>
> **Flexible hour patterns offered.**
> **Good basic rate of pay with bonuses.**
>
> **Experience of customer service and keyboard skills and good telephone manner desirable, but training will be given.**
>
> **Send a CV, stating relevant experience and suitability for this role, to S Smith, Countershift, Mail Order, 3 Mail Order Mall ...**

Beneath the surface of every job advert is the real information, trying to leak out. Some adverts are more obvious than others, but most employers are trying to attract the right applicants and ward off the wrong ones. What assumptions could you make about the real requirements of this job, beyond what is obviously stated?

Some possible assumptions

▨ Call centre work is known to be fairly pressurised with targets for the number of calls made.

▨ You need to be able to focus and cut out the noise from other calls that will be being made around you.

▨ 'Dynamic' and 'motivated' are just code words for persistent and enthusiastic in the face of rejection.

▨ It's likely that they will offer you a telephone interview, if your CV is successful in tempting them – a telephone interview for telephone work is a good way of checking how you sound on the phone.

▨ This job is about communicating at all levels with all kinds of people, so people experience is paramount.

Here's how the CV targeting this work might look. Notice the basic, good essentials of any effective CV and the customisation to this job advert. This is part of the CV that a first year university student sent for this kind of call centre work vacancy.

BEN CAMERON

Home address	**Termtime address**
3 The High Road	**Camden Hall**
Aberdeen	**Stansted University**
Scotland	**Stansted**
Tel: 01333 38899	**Mobile: 09887 766667**
Email: bc@email.co.uk	

A motivated, outgoing marketing student with strong communication and IT skills and experience of high level customer service in retail, keen for the challenge of part-time call centre work.

RELEVANT SKILLS AND EXPERIENCE

Communication skills, proven recently in current market research module of course, to deliver an 'on the streets' market research survey for module assignment – this required perseverance, a sunny disposition and a willingness to tramp the streets in all weathers.

Telephone skills, used for a one-week work placement, to sell space in football programme to local businesses.

Retail skills, developed through part-time Saturday job in a major supermarket.

WORK HISTORY

2002 – 2004   **Food You Like Supermarket**
Starting as a shelf stacker, progressed through counter service and till work to supervisor on delicatessen. This developed customer awareness and teamworking.

2001   **Office Supplies Ltd**
Two-week school placement as office junior – this involved general office duties and inputting orders onto a database.

This is the first half of Ben's CV and you can see that he has hit most of the employer's buttons already, by helping the employer make the connection between his skills and experience and what the employer is implying he needs through the job advert. It is vital that, for any advertised vacancy, you do this sort of matching CV which makes it easy for the employer to shortlist you (choose you out of the many applicants) for the next stage of the selection process. In real terms, your CV just gets you through the door – you still have to do the rest!

Interestingly, a good CV can actually break the door down for advertised or unadvertised jobs, especially when someone wants to make a change into a completely different job area.

Speculative/targeted/career progression CVs

Let me explain exactly what I mean by this. It is quite common for people to want to completely change jobs into a new type of career or occupation. It sometimes feels impossible to make a major change like this, but people find themselves in this situation for many different reasons:

■ They took the first job they were offered, and it has not turned out that well.
■ They had low qualifications so took a basic level job as an interim or 'in the meanwhile' job.
■ They hate their job and know they could be happier doing something else.

A typical scenario might be a school leaver called James who took a job in a chicken processing factory. He started off packing Chicken Kievs and the people were fun and the pay was quite good. Eventually, though, it became a little tiresome and although there were possible chances of promotion, he was just not interested. He decided that as he liked computers he would aim for a new job as a computer technician, but although he was quite naturally skilled with computers, he knew he would need some new qualifications.

James went to evening classes and gained some really good IT qualifications and then thought he was ready to apply for these new types of jobs. He noticed the companies who had been advertising locally so planned to make speculative applications to spark their interest in him. Here's how parts of his CV looked – notice how he makes the most of his transferable skills from his current job, but also makes the most of his new qualifications. His Personal Profile statement is particularly important.

James CV Example

Career Objective
A hardworking, reliable person with strong technical IT expertise and problem-solving skills, seeking a career change into help desk/technical IT support work.

Key Skills and Achievements
Practical/technical skills, developed through recent part-time study for City & Guilds Computer Repair and Maintenance and Diploma in Computer Applications qualifications.

Teamwork skills, proven by food production experience, where working under pressure and to targets is vital.
Problem-solving skills, used on recent courses to troubleshoot faults in computer systems.
Ability to prioritise time, shown by recent study for two parallel courses in one year, alongside full-time work.

Qualifications
2003 – 2004   Stansted College
Study and achievement of two separate City & Guilds courses – one on Saturday morning for a whole year, the other on two evenings a week over the year.

- Achieved City & Guilds Computer Repair and Maintenance certificate covering hardware and software configuration, installation and maintenance of PCs and peripherals.
- Achieved City & Guilds 726 Diploma in Computer Applications covering wordprocessing, spreadsheets and databases in Microsoft applications.

Now that is just the part of James' CV that is making the case for his chosen career change and as you can see, it is very convincing!

No one can get away with churning out the same CV for each job, so make sure your CV is specific to its mission and purpose, and be aware that different occupations might have different CV conventions that you will have to bear in mind. For example, CVs for legal jobs have to be full of evidence with a complete absence of wild claims. They need to look and sound professional and the layout would be quite traditional.

Media, marketing and advertising CVs can afford to be a bit more 'out there' and innovative. They may be printed in colour or on brightly coloured paper. So always remember to match the CV to the employer and the occupation.

CVs on a mission

Here are some key points to consider when sending your CV on a mission:

- Research the employer – check their adverts, see if they have a website.
- Analyse the job adverts – what are they really saying they want?
- Research the career or occupation – what sort of CVs are the norm?
- Try and match yourself against what the career/employer is demanding – check what your particular selling points will be.
- Consider carefully how layout/wordprocessing tricks and uniqueness can make your CV stand out from the pile.

Layout

Even the dullest CV can be improved by a sparkling layout. It's a bit like what they do to second-hand cars in a showroom to make them look as good as new. They polish them and wax them. They valet them and set them up to look their most appealing.

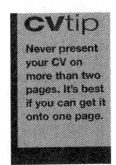

CVtip

Never present your CV on more than two pages. It's best if you can get it onto one page.

Now while appearances are deceptive, you want to create a CV that:

- sounds good – that's the language you use, the customisation, the evidence you give of your suitability
- looks good on paper – that's readable, logical, interesting.

So you have some choices to make on the format. You know you will need certain basic sections, but here is where you have decisions to make. Let's start with headings. Your headings can look like any of the examples below or if you have a desktop publishing package on your computer, you can play around with even more possibilities.

EXAMPLES OF HEADINGS

Headings are normally bold to make them stand out.

Work Experience

Text is left aligned with a border underneath it.

Work Experience

Text is centred.

Work Experience

Heading has a box around it and is left aligned.

Work Experience

Heading has a box around it and is centred.

Work Experience

Heading has a solid block around it, making the text show white. This can be done with different colours, but with the black, it creates a very formal, some would say, funereal look!

If you look back at Sarah's CV (page 36), you will notice that she put border lines between the sections on her CV, which broke up the text quite nicely.

Work Experience

Some people put shading behind the headings, which can be a nice effect:

Work Experience

Most of these features can be experimented with by using Microsoft Word and by clicking on the Format button and going into Borders/Shading.

TEXT TRICKS

Of course you can change the font size and style to help you fit in as much as possible and to make it look good. Steer clear of fiddly fonts and choose the sans-serif fonts like Arial. Arial Narrow is a professional font, which because of its narrowness helps you fit more on the page!

There is some argument about whether to justify the main-body text or not. Justified text for CVs and letters can look smart because it makes a clear white frame around the text. Here is an example of justified text:

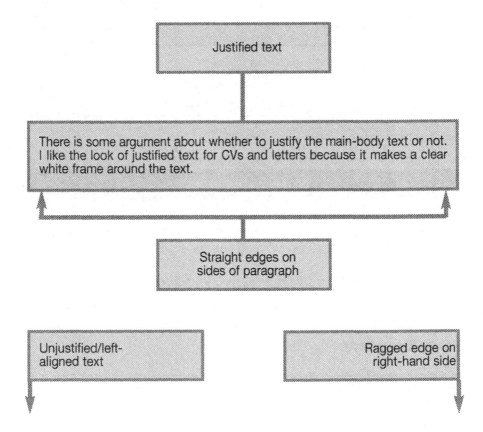

Whether you like it or not one way or the other, I suggest you try it out both ways and then choose. It will depend on your personal preference in the end, but if you want my recommendation, justify each paragraph – it really tidies up the edges!

Alignment and justifying buttons are normally to be found on your toolbar.

MARGINS AND SET-UP

If you find that you are nearly fitting your CV in one or two pages and a line or two is dribbling over to the next page, it is better to try to persuade that extra line or two to join the rest. One way of doing this is to change the margins, which are often set quite generously as a default on the machine. If you go into Page Setup and then click on Margins, you will find the measurements of the left, right, top and bottom margins. I have found that just knocking off a half centimetre top and bottom and left and right, while not affecting the look of the CV, manages to make a little more room for those straggling lines. Try it if you need to get more on to your one and two pages.

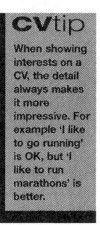

CVtip

When showing interests on a CV, the detail always makes it more impressive. For example 'I like to go running' is OK, but 'I like to run marathons' is better.

Unusual and innovative CV ideas

It is worth giving some thought to ways to make your CV stand out. Here are just a few suggestions of ways you might do this, but use your own imagination and creativity.

One innovative way of presenting your CV is to use a desktop publishing package and make your CV, using the traditional sections, into a tri-fold leaflet – it could look something like this:

Outside of leaflet

Achievements

- Diddleshire rugby team Under 19s captain
- Diddle College football squad captain
- GCSE Maths taken a year early and achieved an A grade
- County standard athlete for 100m and relay

References

Academic
Prof Andrew Diddle
University of Diddle
Diddly Squat Terrace
Diddletown

Personal

Father Alan Griddle
Diddle Parish
Diddletown

Sam Cameron
Diddly Squat Road
Diddly
Diddletown
Tel: 09875 544354
Email: sc@email.co.uk

Inside of leaflet

Inside first fold of leaflet | Middle fold of leaflet | Outside fold of leaflet

Personal Profile

I am a sporty, self-motivated student with strong leadership skills and experience of landscaping, seeking vacation work in construction.

Personal

Clean driving licence
First Aid qualifications

Career Aim

I am aiming for a career in surveying and would value a vacation placement within construction.

Work Experience

2003 – 2004
Diddle Landscapes
Summer vacation work as landscaping labourer working on hard and soft features including drives, patios and rockeries.

2002 – 2003
Diddle Post Office
Saturday work on post office counter.

Education and Qualifications

10 GCSEs A and B grades and two Vocational A-levels in Construction and Engineering

Key Skills

- Leadership and teamwork skills, proven by captaining county and local football and rugby sides
- Strong numerical skills, developed through Vocational A-level study
- Good people skills, shown by Post Office customer service and sporting team interests

This is just one way of presenting your CV and it really looks different, while presenting the information effectively.

COLOUR OF PRINT

If you can afford to use a colour printer to print out your CV, it can be worth considering changing the font colour. Blue print on white paper works well, but this would probably be more suitable for less traditional employers.

YOUR CV AS A SAMPLE OF YOUR WORK

If you are going for something creative, it is useful to use your CV to showcase your talent. Scanned photographs of your work or just the creativity of the way you present yourself can score you points:

- One Fine Art student printed out her CV on her own hand-made paper.
- Some IT students create their CD as a CD ROM with video clips, music, etc. For drama or media students this format could really show off their talents.
- Journalism students might attach an article they have written to their CV.
- Web designers might have weblinks on their CV where the employer can check out the applicant's own work.

INNOVATIVE/WAY-OUT CVs

Really mad or wild CVs can backfire, but here are a few that can actually work:

- One media student sent a CV attached to a pair of oven gloves to a radio station. The first line of the CV explained the oven gloves when it described the applicant as 'Too Hot to Handle'.
- Many art students create a visual CV with photos and drawings and collages.
- Advertising students might write the copy for an advert about themselves.
- Aspiring TV script writers might write a mini play about themselves.
- One applicant wrote his CV on a sandwich board, and wore it to the interview with a rather zany marketing company.

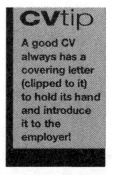

CVtip
A good CV always has a covering letter (clipped to it) to hold its hand and introduce it to the employer!

If you see enough good CVs, you'll begin to get a gut feeling as to what you want from your own CV, but when you critique your own, ask yourself these final questions:

'Have I managed to make a case for my own uniqueness as an applicant?' 'Will an employer know just what I have to offer and how I can make their life wonderful?'

In the next few chapters you will be able to check out CVs for different times and circumstances of your life, so read on.

4

Work experience CVs

They call it 'Catch 22' – how can you get work experience when most employers want you to have work experience? Well, at the school stage, they've pretty much solved this problem by making arrangements with businesses and employers to offer two weeks' work experience to Year 10 or Year 11 pupils. This is sometimes organised through education business partnerships and many employers are happy to be on a database of work experience opportunities for local schools.

Careers co-ordinators/teachers in schools normally organise this and you are encouraged to look at what's on offer. The next stage normally means that you have to specify three choices of work experience as listed on the database. Eventually an offer comes back, normally with a request for you to come for an interview with your CV or to provide a CV prior to interview.

This is usually the first time you have to create a CV and it's made difficult by your lack of life or work experience. Nonetheless, as mentioned before, a good CV can be created with the minimum of information.

Here are the essentials of a perfect work experience CV:

- It is better to try and make it a concise one-page document, than try to fill two pages with waffle.
- It needs to cover three key things: what you are doing currently at school and in your life as a whole, any past or current achievements, and any eventual career aims you might have.
- Some employers like to hear from you about what you are hoping to gain from your placement.

Here's what your standard CV template with the boxes to complete might look like.

Contact details
Name, Address, Telephone number, Email, etc.

Career Aim
If you have any idea what you would like to do in the future then say it here, ideally with your reasons for this choice.

Example
'I am interested in training for pharmacy at university, because my best subjects are Chemistry and Biology and I want to work within the health service.'

If you have no idea what you want to do in the future, then try and focus on a general career area or mention your best subjects.

Example
'I am enjoying English and History best at present and would probably like a job where I could use my skills from those subjects.'

Work Experience Objective
Fill in the gaps here as you think.
'I applied for work with (Employer's name) / I applied for work in (type of work) because it interests me and I would like to know more about it.'

Examples
'I applied for work with Diddle Engineering because engineering interests me and I would like to know more about it.'

'I applied for work in a hotel because it interests me and I would like to know more about it.'

Key Skills and Achievements
Describe what you consider to be your three best skills and achievements.

Current Education

Example
'I am in Year 10 and have just begun my GCSE courses in ... (subjects). I am best at ... (subjects). My predicted GCSE grades at present are C and above.'

Personal
Describe yourself and give an idea of your interests.

Example
'I am a quietly confident person and in my spare time I like reading and going to the cinema.'

Here are three examples of work experience CVs using this model format. CV 1 is for a Year 10 pupil who was asked for a CV prior to interview. CV 2 is for a year 11 pupil who needed to take his CV along to interview. CV 3 is for a pupil who didn't like any of the work experience on offer through school and who decided to try and organise her own work experience, by sending CVs speculatively to her chosen employers.

Background to CV 1

This pupil was rather quiet and shy and wanted to work in a library for her work experience.

EMILY COTTON

3 St Aidans Road, Diddleford
Tel: 09988 454455
Email: ec@email.org.uk

CAREER AIM

I love books and reading and spend a lot of time in bookshops or libraries and have been thinking for some time about a career in librarianship.

WORK EXPERIENCE OBJECTIVE

I'd like to see what it's really like to work in a library. I'd like to work in the Children's Library section.

KEY SKILLS

My best skills are listening and writing. I'd like to develop more confidence in speaking aloud and standing up in front of people. I can do this, but I need to be well prepared.

My proudest achievement is my success at raising money for a local hospice.

CURRENT EDUCATION

I have just started my GCSE courses at St Aidan's School and I like English and languages best.

PERSONAL

I am organised and hard working and in my spare time I enjoy going ice-skating and being with friends. I would like to travel more when I leave school and certainly want to go on to university.

REFERENCES

References available on request.

Background to CV 2

This Year 11 pupil had no career ideas, but had picked a hospital laboratory because he was interested in blood and gore!

OLIVER COTTON

3 Diddlefields, Diddleborough
Tel: 09976 456565
Email: oc@email.co.uk

CAREER AIM

I want to do something interesting and challenging for my career and certainly want to be out and about, rather than stuck in one place.

WORK EXPERIENCE OBJECTIVE

I'm not squeamish and am interested in what goes on in hospital labs. Perhaps I can consider forensics, if it turns out to be interesting to me, but I would definitely like to use my science interest.

KEY SKILLS

I have good problem-solving skills and enjoy working things out. I work well with others and am happy taking the lead.

CURRENT EDUCATION

My GCSE courses are going well, but I need to organise myself soon for my coursework deadlines. My mock exams showed that I need to do more work on subjects that I'm not as interested in. I love Maths, Physics and Chemistry and am taking an extra Statistics class this year.

PERSONAL

I am well motivated and can be logical and analytical, when required. In my spare time I like to use my computer, play chess and score for a cricket team in the summer.

REFERENCES

Available on request.

Background to CV 3

Gina wanted to get some media experience and decided after some research to target local radio stations.

Gina Capaldi
3 Puddle Lane
Puddleton
Puddleshire
Tel: 09988 554343
Email: gina@email.co.uk

Interesting photo of Gina DJing at local fair

I am an enthusiastic, extrovert GCSE student with a passion for radio and two years' experience of hospital radio, seeking any type of work experience in local radio.

What I can offer you

I can write, explain, persuade and do this currently for a local charity magazine and the school newspaper.

Successes - £1000 raised for a hospice through individual canvassing of local businesses and increased number of sales of school newspaper by vigorous and passionate promotion of special offers and competitions.

Hospital radio experience has given me the chance to develop skills and experience in talking to people one-to-one and on air.

Successes – going from ward to ward to check music interests has helped me select music for different tastes, resulting in increased listeners.

Willingness to do the boring and the interesting jobs required, proven by hospice and school newspaper work.

What I'm doing now

School
Studying for eight GCSEs including English, Drama and Media – aiming for A/B grades.
Compete for school in debates and netball.

Outside school
Part-time customer service job at BBB cinemas – great opportunity to watch films, which I can then review for the school newspaper.

Voluntary work

One evening a week at Puddleton Hospital running the evening radio show, playing and presenting a range of music from Sinatra to Oasis.

On hospice committee to produce fundraising magazine.

Eventual Career Aim

I want my own radio show one day, which will have a mix of new music and current issues.

What else do you need to know about me?

I am active and energetic with a strong interest in people and the world around me. I realise how much I still have to learn and experience, and want to start now! I will work hard and enthusiastically.

I have attached some newspaper copy, which can act as references – these quotes are from local events I have helped with.

[Quotes from local newspapers about Gina.]

So that was Gina's CV and you can see that as well as being a rather extraordinary person, she knew how to present herself in an interesting, compelling way to potential employers. Several local radio stations offered her two weeks' work experience on the strength of this CV.

CVtip

A good CV can break the door down for advertised or unadvertised jobs in occupations where there are too many prospective applicants, for example popular jobs in sport or the media.

If you want to have the best work experience placement, here are some final pointers.

Getting the best work experience placement

- As soon as it is announced that you need to pick your work experience, be the first one to go along and check what is available in school – the best placements often go first!
- Decide if you have a particular career choice that you would like to check out – a taster of a job through work experience is really valuable.
- If you don't find the available placements appealing, then ask if you can self-place – this means arranging your own placement.
- For self-placements, do your research and create a CV that will really promote you to those employers.

Working for free on a school work experience is one thing, but a good part-time job can help you earn money outside school, and in the next chapter I'm going to cover the foolproof way to get yourself a brilliant part-time job.

chapter

5

Part-time job
CVs

Many school and college students find that their busy social lives require extra money, which parents/carers may not be prepared to supply. You might decide you need a part-time job for some of these reasons:

- You have an expensive hobby you would like to pursue – hang-gliding, abseiling, etc.
- You need a completely new wardrobe for your new sixth form or college.
- You want to pay for driving lessons.
- You want to go for a holiday abroad with some of your friends.
- You want to make your social life buzz, but it costs.

Before you think of trying for part-time jobs, be aware that there are certain regulations about working hours before the age of 16 years and your school or local education authority can give you information about these. You will find it difficult to gain work before the age of 16 because of these regulations and because employers prefer 16-year-olds – consequently paper rounds and milk rounds are often the only possibilities for under 16-year-olds.

After the age of 16 years, you will have a National Insurance number and strictly speaking you can work full time. However, if you are studying at sixth form or college, you have to make sure that your part-time work does not jeopardise your study and your chances of success at your exams.

Most colleges/sixth forms accept that students will want to work part time but recommend that you limit it to a certain number of hours per week – typically, this might be no more than 10 hours per week, but check with your own college/sixth form.

This generally means that most students between 16 and 18 years can easily manage a Saturday job with one evening tagged on or two or three evenings per week. Usually the kind of jobs that fit this sort of pattern are:

- Supermarket work – stacking shelves after the store is closed and/or counter service/till work
- Department store work – again customer service or cash till work
- Various retail chains on the high street
- DIY superstores – often Sunday work as well as Saturdays
- Farm work
- Vegetable/fruit picking
- Garden centres – nursery work or customer service
- Golf driving ranges

- Leisure centres/gyms – pool lifeguard (if you have the qualification) or leisure centre assistant
- Restaurant/café – waiter/waitressing
- Hotel work and conference service
- Call centre work
- Banking/building society work – often for Saturday morning opening
- Hairdressers
- Car cleaning and valeting
- Cinema complexes
- Fast food restaurants

For most part-time jobs there is a tried and tested method to gain work and it comes down to this – *persistence*.

Students often bemoan the fact that they can't find part-time work, and it generally boils down to two reasons:

1   Not trying hard enough and being crushed by rejection.

2   Setting very high standards for the kind of work they will do.

Here are some important points to be clear about:

- Most students do grotty jobs to earn some cash and generally they don't mind too much.
- Many find that doing a less than perfect job actually motivates them to keep on studying.
- Some find the part-time job surprisingly interesting – it can point them in a career direction that they had not anticipated.

Here's an example – Katie worked for a major retail fashion group on Saturdays and, after her marketing degree, applied to them for a graduate fashion buyer position. Her previous excellent work record and her 'on the ground' understanding of fashion retail made her a convincing and successful applicant for this job.

Suggested gameplan for gaining part-time work

As mentioned before, many try and fail to get work because they get knocked back by rejection. Just count rejection as a lack of appreciation of you and your talents and move on. Here's the gameplan.

1 Decide what kind of work you would like to target.

2 Research who is offering it – ask around and be prepared to walk the streets, walk into shops and other business premises and ask (see 'Asking pointers' below) or telephone many employers.

3 Asking might just generate a job offer or they might say, 'I'm not sure' or, 'I'll have to check', at which point you ask, 'Is it worth me leaving my CV or sending my CV to someone?'

4 One week after sending or leaving your CV, you return there or phone up and ask whether there are any vacancies.

5 If they say, 'Come for an interview', that's good, or if they say, 'No', then ask if something might be coming up or if they know anyone else it is worth contacting.

6 If they have said, 'Try us in a month', follow this up a month later. If they suggest you contact someone else, do so.

It all sounds easy, but it can be a bit gut-wrenching and pride-denting at times, but persistence and your own self-belief will get you through.

Some people avoid this by just sending CVs out to various employers – it can work, but doing it the harder way and actually *asking* often works more quickly.

Asking pointers

Sometimes if you are making calls to employers or dropping in on them, it can help if you have prepared a script and practised it so it is fluent and confident. Here are some examples of ineffective asking:

'Um ... I was wondering if there were any jobs going.'

'Excuse me ... please ... (directed to a shop assistant) are there any jobs here?'

These requests fail because they lack confidence and are just not specific enough.

For telephone calls, you would be better to try something like this:

'Hello, may I speak to the manager? Thank you, what's her name? … Kathy Hartley – that's great … could you put me through to her? Hello, is that Kathy Hartley? My name is Hugo Farnworth and I'm a student at Puddle College doing my A-levels and I am looking for a Saturday job at your DIY Superstore – how could I go about applying?'

Notice that Hugo gets the name of the manager and is specific about what he wants; he doesn't ask, 'Do you have any vacancies?' Instead he confidently asks, 'How do I go about applying?'

For personal face-to-face drop-in visits, something similar would work; it might go like this:

'Hi … (to an employee in fast food restaurant.) I want to know about part-time work here, who should I speak to? (Later, the manager appears.) Hi, I'd like to work here part time at the weekends and perhaps during the week, how do I go about applying?'

Sometimes these techniques will result in an interview, an application form to complete or a request for a CV. CVs for part-time jobs are essentially similar to other good CVs; here are some examples:

CV 1 background

Luke wanted to work at a local racecourse where they had many hospitality events. He phoned up and found out the company that ran the events and then created his CV, having talked to people who worked there already. He had found out that the pay was good, but the work was busy, sometimes stressful and 10-hour shifts were the norm.

LUKE OTIS

3 Puddle Lane, Puddleton, Puddleshire
Tel: 08045 443343
Email: lo@email.co.uk

A reliable, resourceful Vocational A-level Hospitality student with an interest in event management, seeking part-time silver service waiter work.

CURRENT COURSE OF STUDY

Vocational A-level in Hospitality and Catering Management, covering food preparation and service, budgeting, people management, finance, buying and speciality event organising.

KEY RECENT SUCCESS

Themed evenings organised in college restaurant including American, Mexican and Thai cuisine resulted in profit on takings being donated to local charity.

EDUCATION

2002 – present   **Puddleton College**
Vocational A-level Hospitality.
Food Hygiene and Health and Safety at Work certificates achieved.

1997 – 2002   **Puddle High**
10 GCSEs C grade and above achieved.

WORK EXPERIENCE

2002 – present   **Francos Italian Restaurant**
Started on washing up, progressing to waiter and most recently to bar work.

2000   Two weeks' work experience in Puddle Supermarket.

RELEVANT SKILLS

Customer service skills from retail and restaurant experience.
Ability to work long hours under pressure, proven by current part-time work role.
Teamwork skills through basketball interest and through restaurant work in college and Italian restaurant.

PERSONAL

I am energetic and extremely interested in people, and enjoy my current course of study for the chance it has given me to work with other students and the general public. I believe in friendly, courteous service. My eventual career plan is to work in America in hospitality, after studying an event management course at Leeds Metropolitan University.

References available on request.

This CV is very focused and impressive, because it is clear why this student is seeking that part-time work. It will of course add to his CV for the future in terms of valuable experience. Nonetheless, some part-time jobs have little relevance to our eventual career aims and it may seem difficult to be as enthusiastic about a job that may seem rather humdrum. So here's CV 2 which is somewhat vaguer and different!

Background to CV 2

CVtip

Always give examples of what you can do.

Flora just wanted to earn some money and wanted to apply for work at a local nursery for her summer vacation. The work would be quite hard and involved cutting cauliflowers and lettuces and picking tomatoes. She thought it would be OK, because it paid quite well and she liked the idea of getting a tan while working! She designed a fairly simple CV.

FLORA CLARE

3 Treetops Lane, Puddleton, Puddleshire
Tel: 01664 43888 (Home) 07765 332332 (Mobile)
Email: fc@email.co.uk

I am a hardworking, reliable student and I am keen to get some part-time summer vacation work, working outside for a nursery or garden centre. Availability – July to August.

RELEVANT SKILLS AND EXPERIENCE

Shelf-filling work at a local supermarket last Christmas, involving long shifts and physically tiring work – references attached.

Teamwork skills from current Saturday job in fast food restaurant.

High energy levels, proven by GCSE study for exams alongside fast food restaurant shift work.

EDUCATION

1999 – 2004   **Puddle High**
Recently taken GCSE exams in five subjects.

WORK EXPERIENCE

2003 – present   **Chicken To Go, Customer Service.**

2003   Christmas vacation: Puddle Supermarket, shelf-filler.

2002   Two weeks' work experience in a florists.

PERSONAL

I am an outdoor, active person and am keen to swap my current job indoors in the restaurant for a job outdoors in a nursery/growers. I am prepared to be outside in sun or rain.

In my spare time, I go orienteering and hiking.

References from previous employer attached.

So it doesn't have to be a dream job you are applying for – you can still put together an impressive CV that hits all the right buttons for the employer.

At some stage, real life starts and you might have to apply for full-time jobs after GCSEs or after college. The CV format might not be wildly different, but there are ways of making this kind of CV really do its stuff.

6

Real life starts here – first job CVs

This chapter covers first job CVs for 16–17-year-olds and for 18–19-year-olds. First job applications are of course somewhat worrying, mainly because students often start looking for a job just when they are desperate, rather than in a planned-in-advance way. This often means that they apply for anything and everything without much thought and in a rather haphazard way.

Ideally, anyone looking for a job should start at least three months before they need one and for some Apprenticeships or A-level training opportunities, you often have to apply almost a year in advance.

Foundation and Advanced Apprenticeships

Many companies offering Foundation and Advanced Apprenticeships in a range of jobs including business, engineering, construction, hospitality, hairdressing, electronics, sport and leisure advertise these in school and through your local Connexions centre from about December of Year 11.

So typically, you might just have taken your mock exams and will be starting to apply for Apprenticeships. This is good in some ways because you can use your mock exam grades (if they are good!) on application forms or CVs (application forms often ask for your predicted grades).

It can be bad if your mock exam grades are less than brilliant, or if you have not really thought hard about what you want to apply for. This is a time for really good careers advice – see a Connexions Personal Adviser in school, research in the careers library and use careers computer programs like Kudos.

A-level training vacancies

Many students are not aware that many companies offer specific jobs with training to A-level applicants. For example, major banks, building societies, insurance companies, retail groups and the merchant navy have wonderful jobs available for A-level applicants. However, most of these would have to be applied for around October of your second year at sixth form or college, because they have lengthy selection processes that they will put you through.

Will you need a CV at all?

Major organisations offering jobs at 16 or 18 years will often ask you to complete an application form, do an online application form (see Chapter 7 for more about this) or possibly attach a CV to their application form. Smaller companies may ask for your CV. Either way, it is good to compile your CV in about September of your final year at school or college:

- as a way of assembling the relevant information,
- as a way of getting your head straight,
- as a way of making you think about and research just what you want.

So what follows first is a plan of action that you need to set in motion, just when you begin your final year:

1 Research what is out there for you, by way of jobs you would like to do after GCSEs or A-levels. Do this by talking to teachers, your careers teacher and Connexions Personal Adviser (who will be in school regularly), go to careers fairs and Apprenticeship open days and check on the Internet about companies you might like to work for. If you want something unusual, you will have to work even harder!

2 Find out what methods of application are required.

3 Revise really well for mock GCSE or module tests for A-levels or mock A-levels, because these grades will be a way an employer can gauge your motivation and ability.

4 Check deadline dates for applications and stick to these strictly.

5 Create a full CV and complete and send off application forms and/or CVs.

6 Follow up applications and CVs sent by a phone call, about a month after sending them.

So it would be useful to see a typical Year 11 CV and an 18 to 19-year-old CV written for job-seeking purposes.

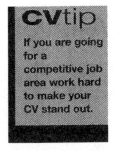

CVtip

If you are going for a competitive job area work hard to make your CV stand out.

Background to CV 1

Will was certain that he wanted to get a job as an electrician after Year 11. He needed to apply for Apprenticeships with the Construction Industry Training Board and with small firms of electricians. His work experience was not particularly useful, as at that stage he had been interested in a job with sport, but he had helped out at school on the technical side for school drama productions.

WILL SKILL

5 Puddle St, Puddlethorpe, Puddleshire
Tel: 0976 44324
Email: ws@email.co.uk

A practical, hardworking GCSE student with strong problem-solving and technical skills, seeking an Apprenticeship as an electrician.

EDUCATION

2001 – present   Puddle High
Currently studying for five GCSEs including English, Maths and Dual Science and Intermediate GNVQ in Engineering.

WORK EXPERIENCE

2004   Puddle Leisure Centre
Excellent reference gained from work as a leisure centre assistant, including exceptional teamwork.

RELEVANT SKILLS

Practical/technical skills through personal interest and developed further through sound production work on two school drama productions, including computer and electronic-based controls.
Customer service skills, proven by leisure centre reception work.

PERSONAL

I have always found electricity fascinating and am regularly being asked to repair computers and electrical equipment for family and friends. I am looking forward to training to be an electrician and using my natural interest and existing skills.
In my spare time, I like to upgrade and repair computers and do motocross.
References available on request.

Background to CV 2

This student had always wanted to be a fashion retail buyer and was hoping that a retail management training scheme after A-levels could lead to that eventually. She needed to complete application forms for the major retail groups but could send a CV as well. She wanted to use her CV to offer additional evidence of her suitability.

Lauren Barton
5 Hobble Street
Puddleton, Puddleshire
Tel: 00088 774436
Email: lb@email.co.uk

Career Objective

I am a bubbly, confident A-level student with a passion for fashion. I am keen to train through a retail management scheme and would hope one day to be a fashion buyer for a major fashion retail group.

Strengths

Ability to stay calm under pressure, developed through exam study and part-time work in a bar.
Interpersonal skills, developed through team captainship for Puddleshire at county standard netball and through Christmas sales work at Puddle department store.
Irrepressible temperament and high energy levels, used currently in children's party organiser work for fast food restaurant.

Education

2002 – 2004	**Puddle Sixth Form**
	Recently taken three A-levels in Textiles, Communication Studies and Psychology – awaiting results, but minimum B grades predicted.
2000 – 2002	**Puddle High School**
	Eight GCSEs achieved, all with pass grades.

Work Experience

Various work undertaken including bar work, retail for department store, children's organiser at fast food restaurant and a milk round, when I was 13 years old. All my work experience has proved that I can work well with others and enjoy contact with the public.

Personal

My interest in fashion is passionate and longstanding. I watch for new trends and keep in touch with ideas from Paris, London or Milan. My future career aim is to be a buyer, but I quite expect to be tempted by other aspects of retail management, particularly marketing, merchandising and personnel. I plan to find out what I am best at and hope to focus my career around that.

In my spare time, I enjoy reading, going to the cinema and live music.

References available on request.

So there are two basic example CVs that can be used as a template for most jobs you decide to go for. However, sometimes a more individualistic CV may be needed to grab attention or make you stand out from the rest, so take a look at the ideas below.

Wacky ways with CVs

For some jobs and careers, there are reasons why you may choose to try a more individual or even crazy CV style.

For jobs where there is intense competition or for jobs that are very popular, you may want to stand out from the other applicants by your choice of CV style.

For jobs that require a more unusual or individual applicant, employers might expect a more innovative and striking CV approach.

CVtip

It's better to show your job and education history in years, rather than state the month and year you started something. For example 2000–2002 is clear enough, rather than September 2000–June 2002

Here are some examples of different CV approaches.

CV IN A PACKAGE

A **packaging design university student** wanted to gain a placement year for his course – he printed his CV onto a piece of packaging he had designed, which was an intricate puzzle box which opened out to reveal his CV. The design of his CV perfectly showcased his skills and creativity.

CV ON A T-SHIRT

An **advertising degree graduate** walked into an advertising company in a major city on a hot day. He was wearing a t-shirt onto which he had printed his CV. He asked the receptionist in a busy concourse area which was surrounded by advertising professionals, 'Can I leave my CV here?' She replied 'Yes'. Revealing a finely toned body, he stripped off his t-shirt and left it on the reception desk. Twenty minutes later he was phoned and invited for an interview.

CV ON A POSTCARD

Now this takes some skill but can mean that you have a CV to send which can have real impact. Using an actual blank postcard or a piece of card the size of a postcard, print out a résumé-style CV onto a postcard – see the example below.

Back of postcard

Dear Mr John Smith, **I am really keen to work for your company as a fitness assistant. I have a range of qualifications in fitness and am currently teaching classes in aerobics and Step. Please see over for details of my experience. I look forward to hearing from you.** **Yours sincerely,** **Jane Foster**	**STAMP** **Employer's name** **Company name** **Address 1** **Address 2** **Town** **Postcode**

Front of postcard

Jane Foster
5 Sussex Garden, Hampton, Essex CO1 7RJ
00077 766889 jfos@hhhh.com

A qualified and enthusiastic fitness coach with experience of work in leisure centres and gyms, seeking job opportunities on cruise liners.

Key Qualifications and Experience
YMCA qualification in cardio-vascular fitness, fitness assessment and teaching of aerobics and Step – 2003
Vocational A-level achieved in Leisure and Tourism plus A-level Human Physiology – 2002

Recent Career History
Currently working for Fitness International as a personal trainer and aerobics teacher

2001–2003
Various experience as a leisure centre assistant for Hampton Borough Council Leisure Services

Personal
I am an extremely passionate fitness coach and love to support people to achieve the best fitness and health levels they deserve. In my spare time, I play hockey, netball and enjoy socialising.

Excellent references available on request

What is particularly useful about this form of CV is that it can make a quick impact and it saves you the cost of envelopes.

CD-ROM CVs

You may have saved your CV to an ordinary floppy disc, but saving it in a CD-ROM version means that you can add music or video clips which could be useful, especially if you wanted to apply for TV presenter jobs or something similar in the media. If you ask an ICT teacher at school or college, you could get some help in creating something really impressive which you could send to media or advertising employers.

YOUR VERY OWN CV WEBSITE

You may be wizard at web stuff or need some help with this, but if you can create your own CV website with you as the focus, you would really be using technology to tempt employers to get to know all about you. You could paste on your regular CV, add pictures of your work or interests, and have video clips of you performing. This is an exciting and compelling way of presenting yourself to a potential employer.

Building your own website can be relatively simple using online website builders such as Yahoo which has around 300 design templates. Some Internet service providers offer free web space (BT/Telewest/Blueyonder) as part of the package. If you want a really professional look then you could use

Microsoft FrontPage for Beginners. Many colleges have evening classes teaching you how to create your own website, so you could check these out too.

Depending on the employer and the career, your own CV website could be a really smart move, offering you a showcase for your personal talents or designs and helping employers find you easily. As well as creating your website, you will need:

- to pay for a personalised domain name, and possibly:
- a link to your site from a good search engine such as Google.

For self-employment or freelance work, in particular, a CD-ROM CV and/or some web space with your name on it could be crucial in advertising just who you are and what you have to offer.

Finally, just remember that these kinds of CVs are more suitable for unusual, competitive or wacky types of jobs or careers. Alternatively, you might want or be required to submit an online CV, so that's what we need to cover next.

7 chapter

Email, online and scannable CVs

The option to email your CV or to make an online CV application can seem quite appealing. The fact that it is fairly immediate may seem a bonus, and there is no doubt that using this method of application can speed up what is often a very slow application process. But it is the very speediness of this method that is in fact a trap for the unwary. This is what happens: Harry Scarry sees a great vacancy on the Internet which asks for a CV to be emailed. He throws together a few details and emails the employer in this way:

'Dear Bravely Construction
Here's my CV as you requested. Hope you like it.
Yours truly, Harry Scarry
PS Open the attachment to view my CV'

Mr Bravely gets a strange email from someone he doesn't know and the header line that announces the CV in his email list has no subject. He doesn't want to open what appears to be a junk email and he never opens the attachment (which is good, because the CV is as unprepared as his email). There's more about email covering letters in Chapter 10, but the point is that the employer doesn't ever get to this CV. The speed of the process has tripped Harry up – this is a wasted opportunity.

Here's another scenario. Marie Scarry sees a great job, which asks her to complete an online CV template or application form. She goes at this with gusto, ploughing through the sections, filling in all the spaces in a blindingly quick way and sends it off. This is received by the employer at the other end with less than enthusiasm, because there are spelling errors and lack of care and thought for promoting her strengths to the employer. She has approached the online CV as a chore to be done rather than as a chance to impress. This is a missed opportunity.

While speed can play an important part in getting your CV to an employer in an instant, don't be fooled into thinking you can get away with a lack of preparation and care. Nonetheless, once you have completed the online CV or emailed your well-crafted CV as an attachment, it will be with the employer in an instant, often allowing a fairly instantaneous response, and that really is the bonus. We all hate waiting for replies from employers and anything that can help speed things up is a benefit.

So let's take some time to ensure that you can use the speed of delivery – email rather than the clichéd snail mail (the postal system) – and the painstaking and effective techniques of crafting a brilliant CV to make a strong impression to get you the job. In simple terms, the speed comes at the end, when you know you are ready, when your CV is ready to roll. The preparation stages may be slow and measured, but they are worth it.

The definitions

Email, online and scannable CV – let's try and clarify exactly what we mean by these rather confusing terms.

Email CVs

Many employers conduct all their recruitment through the Internet and so they may ask you to email your CV. It sounds simple, but it needs some thought to ensure your approach is designed to succeed. At the simplest level, it means what you would think – instead of posting your CV you can email it.

At the most complex level, it might mean that an employer is using specialist software to scan-read your CV to save time. In fact, if your CV doesn't pass the scan, it may never be read by a real person, but de-selected, binned or rejected at the outset! (See Scannable CVs for more on this.)

Requests from Internet job adverts for emailed CVs

If you have your CV ready as a saved document, you can either attach it to an email covering letter or insert a resumé one-page CV inside your email covering letter (an example of this can be found later).

Rules about emailing CVs

There are some sensible rules and conventions about emailing CVs. Take a look at these guidelines:

- The simplest way to do this is to write a formal covering letter email (see Chapter 10) and to indicate an attachment with your CV. However, only do this if you have checked by phone, preferably with that employer, that they are happy to accept your emailed CV and attachment. If they are concerned about virus scares, they may have a policy of not opening attachments from outside sources or they may need to be assured of your virus checker. If they will accept an email, but not an attachment, then you will have to resort to an email letter with a CV within the email letter (example later).

- Email including a résumé-style CV is the second easiest way, as long as you can reduce your two-page CV to a neat and concise one-page CV and reformat it within your email (example to follow).
- If you know or guess that the company will be using scanning techniques to read CVs, then follow their guidelines or the recommended guidelines for scannable CVs which I will cover later.
- An email covering letter is an art in itself, so make sure you follow the advice on these types of letters in Chapter 10.

So, you may find yourself in a situation where you would like to apply speculatively to an employer, and after some research have decided to send a CV within an email. This could be chancy as the employer may choose not to open your email; if you have had a phone contact first, this would be preferable, but even an out-of-the-blue contact might work, if you do it in the right way. Here's an example of a résumé CV within an email, with an 'on spec' or 'on the off-chance' covering email letter:

Example of a CV within an email

Dear Mr Bravely

I am very keen to apply for possible vacancies you might have currently, for work as a construction technician. I have included a résumé CV to highlight my experience, skills and qualifications.

I would like to draw your attention to the fact that I have recently completed a CAD/CAM course through evening study and was thrilled to gain a distinction.

I am happy to attend an interview at your convenience and can bring examples of my work, if you require this.

Yours sincerely

Harry Scarry

HARRY SCARRY

3 Derwent Close, Brentholme BB4 6XX
Tel: 01565 887898
Email: hs@email.co.uk

CAREER OBJECTIVE

A hardworking, reliable person with experience of construction and expertise in CAD/CAM, seeking building/architectural technician work.

KEY SKILLS AND EXPERIENCE

Recent qualification achieved for Vocational A-levels in Construction – all units passed with distinctions and merits.

Vacation work on various building sites, including a number of construction skills such as setting out, hod carrying, labouring, amending plans and costings.

Sporting interests with achievements in football and basketball, with development of leadership and fitness levels.

EDUCATION AND QUALIFICATIONS

1998 – 2002 **Brentholme High**
Four GCSEs passed in Maths, English and Dual Science.

2002 – 2004 **Brentholme College**
Vocational A-levels achieved in Construction covering surveying, architecture, civil engineering, costings, building materials, planning and draughtsmanship.

2003 – 2004 **Rushholme College**
CAD/CAM diploma achieved through part-time study.

WORK EXPERIENCE

2000 – 2004 **Barry Construction**
Starting as a labourer, I have worked most vacations for this small building company, having experience of a range of building skills and working most recently in the drawing office to produce plans and costings.

References – available on request.

This works well to alert the employer to that prospective applicant and it might just generate some interest from the employer. Of course it could be copied and pasted and sent to many different employers, with just a few tweaks.

ONLINE CV (A DIFFERENT KIND OF EMAILED CV)

Some employers, recruitment agencies or specialist job sites will ask you to complete their online CV template or application form. This will look like rather a simple grid. Once completed, you will press a 'send' button and this will be automatically sent through to the employer/agency or site.

RECRUITMENT AGENCIES AND WEBSITES

Various recruitment agencies and websites for jobseekers on the Internet will ask you to complete a CV template online. Check out the Monster board website for an example of this at www.monster.co.uk. You will find that if you want to be emailed suitable vacancies or if you want your CV to be displayed to employers online (with your permission), then you will need to complete their CV template form with the details that *they think are relevant*. This does not allow for a lot of flexibility or customisation.

COMPANY WEBSITES

On individual company websites, they often have an online application form or CV template which they ask you to complete. Similarly, this doesn't allow for much creativity.

ONLINE CV TEMPLATES AND HOW TO DEAL WITH THEM

Just because they are online doesn't mean that you have to do them without preparation. Here are some ideas for dealing with them:

- If you find an online template and you want to make a perfect go of the job, then first print off the template. Somehow, looking at the hardcopy gives you a better idea of how to deal with it.
- Take your own brilliant hardcopy CV and decide which bits of your real CV could fit the space on the online CV.
- Complete the other sections by hand with care and thought.
- Research the company on the Internet, by talking to people who work there, even phone up and ask for shareholder information.
- Decide what key abilities and experience they seem to be looking for and score yourself out of ten as to how well you fit their bill.
- With seven out of ten and over, you are ready to go.

- Open up your own CV on your computer, then minimise it so it is on the bottom toolbar.
- Fire up the Internet site you want and find the CV template they want you to complete.
- You should be able to copy and paste pieces from your own CV into the template – so do this where possible.
- Other sections that ask questions may have to be answered there and then, but you should have prepared these on your hard copy.
- Make sure that every word you use has power to impress and make sure you offer evidence of what you can do and have done.

The Monster website and other similar sites have some good advice on these template CV online forms. Remember the company website forms will work in much the same way.

Scannable CVs

For all sorts of weird and wonderful reasons, recruiters might want to scan your CV. Some employers like to scan CVs using specialist computer software to check if you are the kind of applicant they want – you may email your CV and the first time it is read, it will be read or scanned by specialist software. The scannable format that may be requested just means a CV without fiddly bits and clever formatting features, which will not confuse the rather simple-minded CV scanning software they have.

Some employers have so many applications that they need to sift out the possibles from the impossibles. They will use this CV scanning software that will take the place of a real, live, breathing person and will scan the CVs, looking for key words, to reduce the huge number of applicants to a manageable 'longlist' (the middle stage of selection) before shortlisting.

To do this, they will decide what sort of key words would indicate good applicants; key indicator words might be 'motivated', 'achiever' or 'outgoing', depending on what they are looking for. Often the software is programmed to search for positive nouns like 'leadership', 'manager' or 'success'.

After this first scan, a real person might check through the CVs for the 'through to the next stage' applicants.

Some employers might ask you to send a CV in a particularly scannable format so the software they use can understand it. You will be given instructions to follow to ensure that the software they are using can turn your printed text into electronic format.

Other employers will use scanning software without warning you that they plan to do this!

Whatever, there are two positive ways of approaching this: as a rule, try and make sure your CV is chock-full of words which are compelling and impressive – you have some examples in the CV Power Words list in Chapter 2. Secondly, most employers wanting a scannable CV will tell you so and give you instructions – so heed their advice.

Remember that a CV that you send by post, by email or through an online template may be scanned by that employer, so it is worth paying attention to the way you create your CV, its format and the language you use, if you want to avoid the scanning pitfalls.

SCANNING RULES

Format rules – these are to help the scanner software:

■ Start with your name on its own line at the top, followed by your contact details.
■ Make sure sections are clearly marked with titles like 'Career Objective' or 'Work Experience'.
■ Use Arial or Courier – a font without fiddly bits, ideally in size 12.
■ Leave white space to indicate sections and at the top and bottom.
■ Don't use shading, borders, italics, columns, underlining, bullets or bold – all these prevent the scanner from reading the text.
■ Put spaces between dashes and dates, e.g., 2003 – 04, not 2003-04.

Content rules:

■ This is a simpler, rather classic CV without any wordprocessing tricks to lift it, so the language and phrasing is almost all there is to impress. Use clear language and powerful words to promote yourself as the perfect applicant, always matching yourself and customising your CV to the stated or unstated requirements of each employer.
■ Analyse employer information on their website to track and guess the key words that employer might be scanning for, then use them, if you fit the bill.
■ Keep this kind of CV short and sweet – remember that fewer words often have more impact, so be selective and concise.

SIMPLE SCANNABLE CV EXAMPLE

Here's an example of a previous CV, changed and amended into a scannable CV – it doesn't look quite as impressive, because it is minus the formatting tricks, but it still works well.

Lauren Barton
5 Hobble Street
Puddleton, Puddleshire
Tel: 00088 774436
Email: lb@email.co.uk

Career Objective

I am a bubbly, confident A-level student with a passion for fashion and proven leadership skills. I am keen to train through a retail management scheme and would hope one day to be a fashion buyer for a major fashion retail group.

Strengths

Ability to stay calm under pressure, developed through exam study and part-time work in a bar.

Interpersonal skills, developed through team leadership for Puddleshire at county standard netball and through Christmas sales supervisory management work at Puddle department store.

Irrepressible temperament and high energy levels, used currently in children's party organiser work for fast food restaurant, requiring me to be an excellent organiser and time manager.

Education

2002 – 2004 Puddle Sixth Form

Recently taken three A-levels in Textiles, Communication Studies and Psychology – awaiting results, but minimum B grades predicted.

2000 – 2002 Puddle High School

Eight GCSEs achieved all with pass grades.

Work Experience

Various work undertaken including bar work, retail for department store, children's organiser at fast food restaurant and a milk round, when I was 13 years old. All my work experience has proved that I can work well with others and enjoy contact with the public. Previous employers describe me as an energetic, enthusiastic team worker with a proven ability to overcome difficulties with success.

Personal

My interest in fashion is passionate and longstanding. I watch for new trends and keep in touch with ideas from Paris, London or Milan. My future career aim is to be a buyer, but I quite expect to be tempted by other aspects of retail management, particularly marketing, merchandising and personnel. I plan to find out what I am best at and hope to focus my career around that.

> In my spare time, I enjoy reading, going to
> the cinema and live music.
>
> References available on request.

The key words, which will be picked up by scanning, are those like 'success', 'leadership', 'teamwork' and 'management'. Notice 'captainship' was changed to 'leadership' from the previous CV, because scanning software is unlikely to look for 'captainship'. It is also worth noting that this CV has also delivered 'power words' that a real person scanning the CV will pick up on – for example, phrases like 'passion for fashion' and 'irrepressible' send out great and authentic signals about Lauren.

So to sum up, a scannable CV has to appeal to the scanning software and then to the real person who will be presented with the CV. If you make the mistake of writing the CV solely for the scanner, it could be rather dull and wordy, so use words with care and precision!

Decisions to be made about sending email, online or scannable CVs

Email CV decisions

An employer requests that you email your CV, so you can either:

* write a good covering letter email (an example of this is given in Chapter 10) which has your name, a reasonably formal layout with your reasons for applying and your normal CV (customised to that employer's requirements) as an attachment within the email, or
* you can create a simple one-page resumé CV (in a scannable format, obeying the scannable rules) and place it within your email covering letter.

ADVANTAGES OF ATTACHMENT CV

Your CV arrives the way you want it to, with your layout choices and content.

DISADVANTAGES

Some employers refuse to open attachments from sources unknown to them.

Solution: if an employer asks for an emailed CV, ask if it will be OK to send your CV as an attachment, assure them of your own virus checker and make the subject line of your email say something like 'Emailed CV for (name the job title and ref no) as requested'.

ADVANTAGES OF CV WITHIN EMAIL

If you can place a simple but beautiful CV within a rather brilliant email covering letter, you are close to being a master of the CV writing business. This is the hardest thing to do well, combining the rules of scannable CVs with the precision of a master CV writer! I have shown you how to do this, but it may take practice, blood, sweat, tears and hair loss.

DISADVANTAGES

This type of CV can be rather a meagre thing if it is not bulked up with good language and evidence of your skills and experience.

Solution: résumé CVs within an email have to zing with skills, experience, expertise and strong and powerful key words.

Online CV template decisions

Can you follow instructions? Are you prepared to prepare? Can you use extracts from your current CV within the template? Can you shine despite the restrictions of the online form?

ADVANTAGES

It can be fairly straightforward, once you have done your preparation.

DISADVANTAGES

You can be lulled into a false sense of security by the simple format.

Solution: take your time, do your research, and prepare.

Scannable CV decisions

Are you prepared to rewrite your CV and strip it of its glorious format to impress some software, so that you can skip through a sifting process that may seem wildly unfair?

ADVANTAGES

If you play the game by the scannable rules, you will get through the employer's first sift, which may result in an interview.

DISADVANTAGES

Some scannable CVs are a bit bare and come across as modest and unassuming.

Solution: Practise, rewrite, amend this type of CV until the words sing out!

And finally, another idea – create your own website to showcase your CV

Some clever IT people design their own websites using one of the easy web tools available, and then 'post' their CV in all its glory on their own website. They can then refer people to their website to view their CV and any other examples of their work – pretty nifty!

So, you need to be aware of these new CV types, so that you have additional versions of your CV ready for different types of employers and their recruitment processes. As more and more employers find online recruitment saves them money and time, you will have to be ready to rev up for this new way of accessing jobs.

Let's move on to another life phase that might come your way and think about gap year CVs.

8

Gap year CVs

Mind the gap, stopgap, bridge the gap, close the gap – all these common phrases with 'gap' in them have rather depressingly negative connotations, as if a 'gap' is the last thing we should want. But 'gap' has had a makeover and suddenly 'taking a gap' has become an invigorating, often inspirational thing to do, especially for young people who may often find themselves between stages. So you could be in a gap between sixth form or college and university, or you could take a gap before deciding to go to sixth form or college, or you could take a gap in the middle of a university course or even after university, before starting your real career. Whenever you take your gap, there are strong reasons for doing it and numerous possibilities of how you can spend that time.

Reasons for doing it – what gappers say

- It's not just about lying around and watching daytime TV, it's about living life to the full, trying new experiences, learning new skills, meeting new people *and* having some thinking time about what you really want for your life and career.
- It doesn't have to be something important and worthy that you do – you can go to Indonesia and save the rain forest or stay home, do a humdrum job and tread water while you work out what you want to do.
- It lets you have some growing time and time to explore what's really out there and available for you.
- It's fun to try new things for no other reason than because you want to.
- It's a chance to travel and really get to know countries that a two-week package will never give you.
- You can try out a job to see if it fits and move on if it doesn't.
- You can earn some money to give you some freedom to do things you want to do or to make university easier, if you do go there.
- You may make new friends and learn more about yourself than you could ever guess.
- You could develop new skills like resourcefulness, money budgeting, independence.

- You may chance upon some interesting activity or experience which will give you some clues towards a future career.
- And lastly, gapping can look really good on your CV if you can present and promote it in the right way.

Numerous gap possibilities

It's hard to say just what you couldn't do in a gap year, but here are a few examples and ideas and weblinks to good gap year work:

Study abroad in another country – try **www.aaiuk.org**.

Study in Italy – try **www.arthistoryabroad.com**.

Youth work experience (unpaid) in Africa for four or five months – try **www.aventure.co.uk**.

Conservation experience on game reserves in Africa – try **www.ConservationAfrica.net**.

Young explorers expeditions to Greenland or the Himalayas – try **www.bses.org.uk**.

Summer camp work in America – try **www.bunac.org**.

Sailing, diving, windsurfing training in Greece – try **www.flyingfishonline.com**.

More expeditions – **www.raleigh.org.uk**.

Voluntary work in this country through your local Council for Voluntary Service, Millennium Volunteers or through Community Service Volunteers – try **www.csv.org.uk**.

Work for a company gaining skills prior to university through the Year In Industry scheme – try **www.yini.org.uk**.

Learn acting techniques and directing and end up at the Edinburgh Festival – try **www.yearoutdrama.com**.

Also check out **www.gapyear.com** and **www.yearoutgroup.org**.

These are just a few of the formally organised possibilities, but you could organise your own timetable and do a mixture of things or just one job or activity. Here are two examples of gap time well spent.

After A-levels, Sophie wanted to have a year out of study to have some fun and travel a little. She worked for three months in a pub to earn some money.

Then she went to a ski resort for the winter as a travel rep, then she worked for the summer in France at a campsite. She gained lots of experience, travelled a bit and earned some money.

Amanda wanted to go to Australia so she had a two-year gap. In the first year she worked in an insurance office and earned her flight and spending money for Australia. The second year she spent travelling till her money ran out.

Whatever kind of gap you plan, be warned that gapping is quite addictive, and when real life beckons, it can be hard to swap gapping for a more everyday lifestyle!

However, there are ways of allowing your gapping to create new work possibilities and point in directions that you might not have expected. It may be that you might not need a CV to secure yourself your desired gap time, but a CV may be useful in a number of key areas:

- to get yourself a job to earn the money to go gapping – a pre-gap CV
- for a between college and university gap – a CV for pre(university)-gappers
- to have ready to apply for ad hoc jobs while you are gapping – the Earn-quick-money gap CV
- the mid-university-course gap CV – the I-just-need-a-break gap CV
- the CV for someone wanting to take a break after university – the post(university)gap CV.

Here are three examples of the same person's CV, amended and tweaked for different gap times. What this shows is that gapping is contagious – this person gapped before university, mid-way through and then after university. Now working for a large travel company, arranging tours, all his experience was undeniably relevant.

The first CV is his initial version, which actually gained him his first job in a pensions company shortly after he finished A-levels.

SAM SCOTT

33 Harris Terrace, Newboro NN55 6BD
Tel: 06565 455554
Email: sc@email.co.uk

I am a confident, sporty A-level student with strong numerical and communication skills, seeking interesting work in financial companies.

KEY SKILLS

Self-motivation and leadership skills, proven by sporting performance – personal bests at county level athletics and team captain of college rugby team in national Sevens competition.

Numerical skills, developed through GCSE Higher Maths and Statistics course.

Communication skills, used currently in a busy hotel bar, for customer service and working well with other staff.

EDUCATION

1996 – 1998   **Newley Sixth Form College**
Four A-levels achieved in Maths (B), Statistics (A), History (B) and Economics (B).

1995   **School Industry Day award winner**

1991 – 1996   **Newley High**
Eight GCSEs achieved including Maths, English, Science, History and Business Studies.

WORK EXPERIENCE

1995 – present   **The Plough and Harrow at Newley**
Starting as glass collector, progressing to food service and then bar work.

1995   **County Council Surveying Department**
Two weeks' school work experience, measuring and taking notes for surveyors, including basic office work and filing.

PERSONAL

I am an active, energetic person who enjoys meeting people and motivating others. I have to do this in my role as rugby captain and when working part-time in a busy hotel, when I have to train new student staff.

I have always been interested in money and would like to help people manage their money in a banking, building society or insurance area. I think my quick numerical skills and my customer service experience will help with this.

In my spare time, I enjoy rugby, basketball and cricket and I would like to travel more in the future. I hold a current driving licence and have passed Health and Safety and First Aid certificates through my part-time job.

References available on request.

This CV worked to help him earn some money to go travelling to Australia. He worked in pensions for about 10 months (it wasn't really his dream job, but he did well at it and it paid quite well) and then he set off travelling.

He next needed a CV when he was running short of money in Australia and needed to supply one to an agency for some quick-money work. He didn't have to change it much, but he highlighted his bar/hotel work and explained his travel plans, and reduced it to a rather simple version, which was perfect for the recruitment agency purposes. This is how it looked.

SAM SCOTT

Bacpackers Hostel, Ozley
Email: sc@email.co.uk

A confident, sporty, active, energetic student with experience of bar/hotel work and an ability to stay calm when working under pressure.

WORK EXPERIENCE

1998 – 1999   **Harry Pensions Group – Telephone pensions advice service.**

1996 – 1998   **The Plough and Harrow Hotel and Restaurant, Newley**
Starting as glass collector, progressing to food service and then bar work. Experience in the following:

- Silver service waiting
- Basic food preparation
- Bar work including cocktail bar
- Hotel reception and bookings.

1995   **County Council Surveying Dept**
Two weeks' school work experience, measuring and taking notes for surveyors, including basic office work and filing.

EDUCATION AND QUALIFICATIONS

I hold a current driving licence and have passed Health and Safety and First Aid certificates through my previous part-time job.

1991 – 1996   GCSEs and A-levels achieved in Newley, UK and unconditional university place gained.

PERSONAL

I am an active, energetic person who is hardworking and reliable. Working part-time in a busy hotel, I had to be flexible and ready to help out in a number of areas and deal with demanding customers in a tactful way.

In my spare time, I enjoy rugby, basketball and cricket and I plan to travel on to New Zealand after working in Sydney for three months.

References available on request.

Two years later, he was back studying at university and decided that a gap year for the third year of his course might be useful. He wanted to earn some money to pull back his overdraft and ideally get paid while he travelled. He wanted to apply to European campsite holiday companies and decided to send a CV to ask about possible vacancies for the summer. This is how he customised his CV for that job opportunity.

SAM SCOTT

Newboro University Hall, Newboro NW99 7PD
Tel: 06655 443225
Email: sc@email.co.uk

A confident, sporty, active, energetic student with experience of bar/hotel work and gap year travel through Europe and Australia, seeking summer vacation work in Europe.

RECENT TRAVEL EXPERIENCE

1999 – 2000   One year spent travelling through Europe and then on to Australia and New Zealand.

SKILLS AND EXPERIENCE GAINED

* Ability to be resourceful and use initiative, when luggage went missing and when travel arrangements were changed by travel company.
* Ability to build rapport quickly with different people and nationalities and to develop good relationships.
* Willingness to do whatever it takes to sort things out, proven on numerous occasions in travel schedule, when travel connections did not materialise or were cancelled.
* Interest and enthusiasm for other countries and people.

WORK EXPERIENCE

1999 – 2000   Various part-time work undertaken while travelling including picking and boxing mandarins, bar and restaurant work.

1998 – 1999   **Harry Pensions Group – Telephone pensions advice service.**

1996 – 1998   **The Plough and Harrow Hotel and Restaurant, Newley**
Starting as glass collector, progressing to food service
and then bar work. Experience in the following:
- Silver service waiting and basic food preparation
- Bar work including cocktail bar
- Hotel reception and bookings.

EDUCATION AND QUALIFICATIONS

I hold a current driving licence and have passed Health and Safety and First
Aid certificates through my previous part-time job.

2000 – present   Newboro University, studying Hospitality and Tourism.

1991 – 1998   GCSEs and A-levels achieved.

PERSONAL

I am an active, energetic person who is hardworking and reliable. I am keen to
gain summer vacation work in Europe on a campsite. My hotel and bar
experience proves that I can be flexible and deal with customers in the most
helpful way.

In my spare time, I enjoy rugby, basketball and cricket.

References available on request.

So Sam was successful at gaining work in Europe for the summer and then
returned to university and completed his degree. After finishing his degree he
wanted to work for a year teaching English abroad to give him the chance to
polish up his Spanish.

SAM SCOTT

Newboro University Hall, Newboro NW99 7PD
Tel: 06655 443225
Email: sc@email.co.uk

A confident, sporty, active, energetic student with experience of gap year travel through Europe and Australia and vacation work in Spain, seeking English teaching work in Spain.

RECENT EXPERIENCE

Working in Spain on a campsite with various nationalities as customers, I developed an interest in speaking European languages and taught myself Spanish, while practising constantly.

WORK EXPERIENCE

2002	Five months' work in Barcelona for major camping operator.
1999 – 2000	One year spent travelling through Europe and then on to Australia and New Zealand.
1999 – 2000	Various part-time work undertaken while travelling including picking and boxing mandarins, bar and restaurant work.
1998 – 1999	Harry Pensions Group – Telephone pensions advice service.
1996 – 1998	**The Plough and Harrow Hotel and Restaurant, Newley** Starting as glass collector, progressing to food service and then bar work.

EDUCATION AND QUALIFICATIONS

2000 – 2004	**Newboro University** Achieved degree in Hospitality and Tourism 2:2.
1991 – 1996	GCSEs and A-levels achieved in Newley, UK.

I hold a current driving licence and have passed Health and Safety and First Aid certificates through my previous part-time job.

PERSONAL

I am an active, energetic person who is hardworking and reliable. I am keen to teach English as a foreign language in Spain to use my existing skills and develop my experience further.

In my spare time, I enjoy rugby, basketball and cricket.

References available on request.

So, that's how one CV can change and grow and become what you need it to be. One last thing on gapping – it's how it changes your life and your own desires and motivations that really counts, not just how it changes your CV.

University student CVs – how to earn while you learn

You've probably heard enough about poverty-stricken students who have to take jobs to get through. You've probably also heard that university students have a great time and that having a great time costs. You might be a student now, wondering how you can afford to have a good time, manage your student loan, your overdraft and study as well.

Well, here's some good news! It's actually not that hard to work, earn and study and it's really good for you! It does take determination, some effort and preparation, but it is possible to work term time for social money and in the vacations to prop up the next year's spending or to bring the overdraft down a little. And all this will be good for you, because it will make you *employable*, that magic word employers use to describe someone that they want to employ.

Why is it good for you?

Many students still leave university with a degree but not much else by way of proof that they can work and be useful to an employer. Along with job-specific skills that employers want such as business, construction, nursing, surveying, engineering, computing skills or whatever skills are required for the job they offer, employers want general skills like evidence of reliability, flexibility, a confident attitude, teamwork, etc. So any part-time or vacation work can give you mountains of evidence of these general skills, and this is often what gets you that brilliant graduate job.

What kind of part-time jobs do students get?

Probably the most popular part-time student jobs are bar work and retail because they offer flexible working patterns that fit around lectures, etc. Most universities have a student job shop, which is a great source of part-time work.

There could be term-time jobs available in offices, call centres, garden centres, leafleting, etc or one-off jobs in mailshotting, marketing, sales, interpreting, translating, etc. A one-off job might be with a company that wants a student for a week to fill envelopes. Within the universities' Prospects website, www.prospects.ac.uk, there is a section for part-time jobs for students run by Hot Recruit, which offers some more unusual possibilities. Recently, they had vacancies for wingwalking – that is, standing on the wing of an aeroplane while it is flying!

It is quite possible to get the most amazing work experience while you are studying, through a mixture of part-time jobs and vacation work. One typical student started with a fast food job part-time, then moved onto retail work at weekends, then took some leafleting work from the student job shop, then gained two weeks' work in the Easter vacation data inputting in an office, then six weeks' work in the summer on a building site, then Christmas work delivering letters!

Your university careers service can also be a good source of part-time or vacation work – they can refer you to websites which list good work opportunities while you are at university or once you go home. An example of a good website for vacation and part-time jobs for students is NWSAGO at: www.nwstudentandgraduate.ac.uk.

CVs for part-time work

You might not need a CV for part-time work, as you might just be asked to ring up. But it's useful to have one ready. Here's a first example.

Susie was studying fashion design and wanted to apply for some part-time work on a project for six weeks with a local jeans manufacturer. It involved flexible hours, but they wanted to hear from students with skills in embroidered design for jeans. Susie had little experience of this, but tried to show transferable skills and a willingness to learn.

SUSIE TRANTER

Fallowfield, Marsh Lane, Duddleton, Duddleshire DD87 9BD
Tel: 07799 456465; **Email:** suslet@aol.co.uk

I am an outgoing, creative fashion student with expertise in design and experience of the textile industry, seeking part-time project work in a design company.

KEY SKILLS AND EXPERIENCE

Creative skills, used currently on fashion degree course and in part-time job in art and craft shop, where I run workshops for children on macramé, patchwork and machine embroidery.

Textile experience from vacation work as a sewing machinist in a curtain and bedwear manufacturing company.

Ability to work on own initiative or in a team, proven by current and previous work experience.

EDUCATION

2003 – present	**Duddleton University** Currently studying degree in Applied Fashion Design with Textiles modules.
2001 – 2003	BTEC Textile Design and BTEC Foundation Art achieved with distinctions overall.
1997 – 2001	Four GCSEs achieved in English, Geography, Art and Drama.

WORK EXPERIENCE

2003 – 2004	Part-time retail assistant in Duddleton department store, working in young fashion departments offering customer service and dealing with orders. Saturday work.
2003 – 2004	Sunday work at Art and Craft Superstore, offering craft workshops to young children.
2003	Summer vacation work as sewing machinist at Duddleton Fabrics – this was target driven and required teamwork to produce orders on time.

2002   One week's work experience in Art and Craft Superstore.

PERSONAL

I have proven myself to be hardworking and reliable in my weekend jobs and would love the chance to experience work in a real fashion company. I am very interested in machine embroidery and its applications and this would help me select my advanced degree modules. I am very wiling to learn and know that I am a quick learner.

References available on request.

Susie used an embroidery type style underneath her headings to customise it to that employer and made a clear point that she is 'willing to learn' and a 'quick learner'.

Vacation placements

Susie's type of CV would work very well for the kind of vacation placements that are offered by many major companies. These are more often for students who have a clear idea of what they want to do at the end of their degree, and might be in business, accountancy or engineering. Check with your university careers service for details of these, which are often advertised in the September before the summer vacation placement starts.

Just any job CVs

If you just need to earn money fast, then a less specific CV is needed, which can be used for various part-time or vacation jobs. This is how Susie's CV might look if she wanted to keep it more general:

Susie Tranter
Fallowfield, Marsh Lane, Duddleton, Duddleshire DD87 9BD
Tel: 07799 456465; Email: suslet@aol.co.uk

I am a hardworking, outgoing, creative fashion student with strong communication skills, seeking part-time work.

Key Skills and Experience

Creative skills, used currently on fashion degree course and in part-time job in art and craft shop, where I run workshops for children on macramé, patchwork and machine embroidery.

Textile experience from vacation work as a sewing machinist in a curtain and bedwear manufacturing company.

Ability to work on own initiative or in a team, proven by current and previous work experience.

Education

2004 – present	**Duddleton University** Currently studying degree in Applied Fashion Design with Textiles modules.
2002 – 2004	BTEC Textile Design and BTEC Foundation Art achieved with distinctions overall.
1998 – 2002	Four GCSEs achieved in English, Geography, Art and Drama.

Work Experience

2003 – 2004	Part-time retail assistant in Duddleton department store, working in young fashion departments offering customer service and dealing with orders. Saturday work only.
2003 – 2004	Sunday work at Art and Craft Superstore, offering craft workshops to young children.
2003	Summer vacation work as sewing machinist at Duddleton Fabrics – this was target driven and required teamwork to produce orders on time.
2002	One week's work experience in Art and Craft Superstore.

Personal

I am keen to gain part-time work which I can fit in around my studies. I can be flexible and am willing to learn new skills. I can work well with others or on my own initiative, as has been proven by my current weekend jobs.

In my spare time I enjoy sewing and designing. I hold a current driving licence.

References available on request.

So, I hope you now realise that it is perfectly possible to earn money when you need to through part-time or vacation work or a mixture of both, and remember that all this additional experience can be used on a future CV to show employability and evidence of your skills and abilities.

Every CV needs a friend – and that's the covering letter, so let's find out what makes the perfect covering letter.

10

Covering letters

Remember your first party when you were a small child? You had the invitation and you started getting excited about going to your friend's house. When you arrived there, things started to change – everything looked strange and unfamiliar and you suddenly felt the urge to grab your mum or dad's hand for safety as you walked into the party.

Well, think of a covering letter as the clasp of a hand for the CV as it makes its way to an employer. The covering letter makes the introductions and assures the CV of a warm welcome. Without a covering letter, the CV is a bit shaky and may even be ignored.

Employers complain about receiving unsolicited CVs all the time and these are particularly perplexing if they arrive in an envelope with no explanation. An employer has no way of guessing just what the CV is really for, unless there is an accompanying letter to explain. If you are going to send a CV 'on spec', the only chance it has is if you write a compelling, professional covering letter.

The covering letter acts as an encouragement to the recruiter – it says 'Read the CV!' If the letter seems interesting, the employer may be tempted.

Because you want the employer to really take time on your CV, the covering letter needs to:

- be short and punchy
- be no more than three paragraphs
- say what you want
- say what you are offering.

Some covering letters are there to accompany CVs or application forms for openly advertised jobs, so these have to refer to the advert and its reference number, if it has one.

Some covering letters are 'I wonder if' letters, which are trying to uncover any hidden jobs that might be available.

Some covering letters are actually an email that offers your CV as an attachment, or an email letter which contains your resumé CV (as mentioned in Chapter 7).

The best way to make this clearer is to discuss these three types of letters in detail, with some examples, so let's start.

Straightforward covering letter to accompany a CV for an advertised job

Job adverts often ask you to 'send a CV and covering letter'. Your CV has to show you have understood the key points of the advert and the subtext (what the employer is suggesting) and your covering letter has to say roughly the same and offer something unique about you, ideally.

It is a good idea to read any additional information the employer sends out, if it is available, because there are always important subtext clues in this information. Subtext is the 'beneath the surface' message the employer is offering; for example, here are some typical phrases from job adverts with their subtext translation alongside:

'Bright, motivated, self starter' – equals happy, clever, can work on own initiative, can take the ball and run with it, etc.

'Can look forward to the challenge of working in a fast moving environment' – 'challenge' can mean dealing with problems, difficulties and stretching yourself; 'fast moving environment' can mean busy and/or pressurised.

Even bland phrases have a subtext – 'good working knowledge' means that you have to be able to say 'I can do that', 'enthusiastic and dependable' means that you have to lay claim to these qualities and offer some proof.

What the advert or the accompanying information gives you has to be analysed, so that you can decide firstly whether you fit the bill and secondly whether you have evidence to prove it. Here's a job advert analysed to show you how:

CREDIT CONTROL ADMINISTRATOR

Norman Gregson Collection Sports Fashion Clothing
With a good working knowledge of credit control and
excellent communication skills, we need a bright,
motivated self-starter to work in a small team.

If this role interests you, you must be excited about joining
a team who value hard work and commitment.

**Send your CV and covering letter quoting Ref No. 99877
to Frances Ford ...**

To hit all the right buttons, your CV will have to give details of all the following;

- that you are happy and pick things up quickly
- that your best skill is being able to communicate
- that you can work on your own initiative
- that you like hard work and are committed to high standards
- that you are enthusiastic (excited).

You will use the initial profile or career objective to suggest 'hardworking and enthusiastic'. You will show communication skills in the 'Key Skills' section with an example of when you use these skills. You will refer to your happy temperament, your high standards, your motivation, etc in the final personal section. Remember that wild claims like 'I set myself high standards' or 'I am an excellent communicator' are pointless, unless you can use evidence to back this up. So you might say:

'I like to give 100% to my work and this was rewarded in my last job with a retail assistant of the month award,' or

'I used my communication skills for my sociology coursework, doing market research on the streets of Duddleton, persuading shoppers to stop and answer 20 questions about their buying habits.'

Your covering letter will have to hint at the same things and encourage the reader to read your CV for more in-depth proof of your suitability.

Let's take a look on the next page at an example covering letter, which is aiming to fulfil the obvious and less obvious requirements of the previous sample job advert.

Harvest Home
Harvest Walk
Duddleton
Duddleshire DD4 GG6

Frances Ford
Norman Gregson Sports Fashion Clothing

3 March 2004

Credit Control Administrator post ref no 99877

Dear Frances Ford (or Dear Madam)

I was delighted to see your job advert in the Duddleton Echo for the post of Credit Control Administrator, because I have the skills and experience to do this job well. My previous role in credit control with a mail order company developed my skills in credit procedures and in my current customer service role, I have to use my communication skills to help customers manage their accounts and their debts, if required.

I can offer a calm and happy disposition, an ability to work without supervision and within a team situation, and a committed, hardworking attitude, proven by references from my current and previous job roles. In addition, I believe that my current experience in a busy call centre environment has prepared me to deal with challenge and pressure.

I have always wanted to work for a sports fashion group and would love the chance of an interview to prove my suitability further. I attach my current CV and look forward to meeting you.

Yours sincerely

Hannah Cameron

Hannah Cameron

Att: Curriculum Vitae

The problem with letter writing for job adverts is that it isn't the same as the letter you were taught to write at primary school. Those rather sweet handwritten letters with paragraphs indented (start of paragraph going in a space) will not make a good impression for job applications, so here are the guidelines for a professional, business-like letter for application purposes.

Your address first

Your address should be at the top left. You don't need to put your name or telephone number, as these are on your CV.

Name of employer

The name and company name of the employer should come next, in exactly the way it is written in the advert. If the advert reads, 'Mr T Simpson, Wellliving Products', you will put exactly this at this point in the letter.

Job title and ref no

If they have offered a reference number use it, but it is always worth identifying clearly the job you are applying for, in this way.

Dear ...

It is perfectly correct to call them by their full name, if they have offered it in the job advert, so 'Dear Frances Ford' would be correct or the more formal 'Dear Madam', *but* it would be 'Dear Mr Simpson' or 'Dear Sir' if you were applying to Wellliving Products.

A VERY IMPORTANT POINT

If you go for 'Dear Frances Ford' or 'Dear Mr Simpson' you would finish with 'Yours sincerely', *but* if you go for 'Dear Sir' or 'Dear Madam' it will always be 'Yours faithfully'.

The strong start

Too many letters start in a really dreary way – for example:

'With reference to your advert ... I would like to apply' ... or

'I wish to apply for the job advertised on Wednesday 5 April'.

It is much better to try and infuse the first line with some enthusiasm, so try

'I am keen to apply for the post of ...' or

'I am delighted to apply for ...'

This is especially important when the job advert is asking for an enthusiastic person!

First paragraph

This first section hits the employer with the relevance of the applicant's experience and skills in a powerful way. It is answering the questions of the employer who might be reading this letter. The employer is wondering, 'What can this person offer me? Have they got what I want?'

Second paragraph – matching analysis of subtext

The applicant shows that she has really read the advert, by matching her skills and qualities to what the employer is asking for.

NOTE – the 'In addition ...' sentence in this paragraph is a great way to highlight some special or unique experience you have. You should aim to show something unique in your letter and draw attention to it, starting a sentence with 'In addition ...' or 'Furthermore ...' or 'What's most important is ...', as this gives the letter more impact.

Third paragraph – strong finish

Notice the enthusiasm for working for that employer – it's always good to give the employer a positive stroke. This also shows self-belief that she can prove that she is the right person for the job and the implied assumption, 'I'm sure you'll want to meet me.'

Att:

This is an abbreviation for an attachment and is a business-like way of saying, 'Now read my CV!'

So that's a straightforward covering letter example, but what if you remembered seeing adverts in the past for a particular company and were interested in working for them? Your speculative CV would need a slightly amended covering letter. Let's pretend you were interested in working for the same sports fashion company, but they had not advertised. If you had been smart, you might have saved previous adverts and have the name of the person to contact, or you might have done some research by phoning the company and asking who dealt with recruitment. Whatever, here's what the letter might look like – notice the minor changes from the first letter.

Covering letter for speculative applications

Harvest Home
Harvest Walk
Duddleton
Duddleshire DD4 GG6

Frances Ford
Norman Gregson Sports Fashion Clothing

3 March 2004

Dear Frances Ford (or Dear Madam)

I am very keen to apply for possible vacancies with your company within customer service or credit control. I am currently working in a busy call centre environment helping customers manage their accounts and their debts, if required. My previous role in credit control with a mail order company developed my skills in credit procedures.

I can offer a calm and happy disposition, an ability to work without supervision and within a team situation, and a committed, hardworking attitude, proven by references from my current and previous job roles. In addition, I believe that my current experience in a busy call centre environment has prepared me to deal with challenge and pressure.

I have always wanted to work for a sports fashion group and would love the chance of an informal chat to discuss any work possibilities with your company. I attach my current CV and look forward to the chance of meeting you.

Yours sincerely

Hannah Cameron

Hannah Cameron

Att: Curriculum Vitae

As you can see, the same good points from the first letter are used again. The letter has a good, professional look. It shows enthusiasm and a positive promotion of what the applicant has to offer, and has a strong finish. Some applicants might follow up this letter by a phone call a week later to check about work opportunities.

Here is a template for a good, speculative covering letter that you can use and tweak for your own purposes.

Speculative covering letter template

Your address
Your address
Your address

Name of employer contact
Name of company/organisation

Date

Dear (Name of employer or Sir/Madam)

First paragraph with strong start – why you are applying
I am keen to apply for possible vacancies in … , because …

Second paragraph – what you are offering
I can offer … (mention work experience or transferable skills)

Final paragraph – strong finish
I have always wanted to work in ... and would love the chance of an interview to prove my suitability further. I attach my current CV and look forward to meeting you.

Yours sincerely

(Sign here)

Your name

Att: Curriculum Vitae

Good covering letters always have certain important features:

- They look good and are business-like, professional and printed out on the same quality paper as your CV – cream or white paper for most traditional jobs.
- They sound good, with clear language that promotes what you have to offer.
- They are customised to the stated or unstated needs of that employer.
- They highlight something unique that you can offer, ideally.

Now let's think about email covering letters and their peculiar rules and conventions.

Email Covering Letters

In many ways these are simpler than other letters, as there is no need for your own contact details and they are very immediate. Nonetheless, the very informality of email letters can be a trap. You need to aim for a relatively formal, professional letter within the email constraints. It can be short and snappy, but needs something to 'hook' the interest of the reader, whether it is speculative or requested. Here are two examples, one for an advertised vacancy and one sent 'on spec':

Covering letter for an advertised job

Dear Frances Ford

I am keen to apply for the post of Sales Order Processing Administrator, because I have had a longstanding interest in working for your company and because I believe I have the skills and experience you need.

I have recently completed Vocational A-level courses in Business Studies, which included Sales and Marketing and in my part-time work for a major retail department store I have gained experience of customer service and placing customer orders.

I have excellent computer skills, being familiar with Microsoft Word, Excel and Access. I am motivated and reliable and would love the chance of a challenging sales processing role. Please consult my CV attachment for further evidence of my skills and experience. I look forward to hearing from you.

Yours sincerely

Hannah Cameron

Hannah Cameron

Att: Curriculum Vitae

What you will notice about this email covering letter is that it is a slightly abbreviated version of an ordinary covering letter. It has shorter paragraphs, which are easier to read on screen, but it hits the same buttons in terms of positive promotion of skills and experience.

Here's the same letter but with a speculative angle.

Speculative Email Covering Letter

Email	
From:	Provider Name
	Hannah Cameron
To:	francesford@normangregson.co.uk
Subject:	Job vacancies in administration with your company

Reply   Reply All   Forward   Delete

Dear Frances Ford

I am keen to apply for possible vacancies within your company in administration or sales processing, because I have had a longstanding interest in working for your company and because I believe I have the skills and experience to work well for you.

I have recently completed Vocational A-level courses in Business Studies, which included Sales and Marketing and in my part-time work for a major retail department store I have gained experience of customer service and placing customer orders.

I have excellent computer skills, being familiar with Microsoft Word, Excel and Access. I am motivated and reliable and would love the chance of a challenging administration or sales processing role. Please consult my CV attachment for further evidence of my skills and experience. I would appreciate the chance of an informal chat with you to discuss any possible opportunities with your company. I look forward to hearing from you.

Yours sincerely

Hannah Cameron

Hannah Cameron

Att: Curriculum Vitae

Again, with just a few amendments, this is a fairly similar letter, but it still acts in a very clear and positive way.

Here's just one more email letter, which was sent 'on spec' to various advertising companies – it is a little 'out there' but works for the industry it is targeting.

Reply   Reply All   Forward   Delete

Dear Brian Hewitson

I want to work for you and I can cost you nothing! I am a motivated and creative advertising student, determined to gain a summer vacation placement working for an advertising agency. I will make tea, photocopy or do vast mailshots, but it would be an even better use of my time if you let me write copy or work on a project to media plan.

My current course has been amazing so far and has covered the creative and the business side of the advertising industry, but I need real-life experience and am willing to forgo the chance of earning big money this summer, doing something I hate, to work for you doing something I love, making you money and gaining some valuable experience at the same time!

Take a look at my CV attachment and you'll find the evidence that will prove to you how useful I can be. I can work for eight weeks from July to August. I will phone you in a week to hear what you think and/or set up an appointment with you.

Yours sincerely

Hannah Cameron

Hannah Cameron

Att: Curriculum Vitae

This letter is full of self-belief and vitality, but more than that she has made a strong case to tempt the employer to open the attachment!

So that's probably all you need to know about covering letters. Here are some final thoughts:

- Your CV is just a means to an end really, just a way of saying 'Look at me – I want to work for you'.
- Your approach to CV and letter writing tells an employer a lot about you – research and attention to detail really pay off!
- Being passive and waiting for things to happen rarely works – be proactive in the application process and set yourself targets of how many CVs you will send off each day and then how many phone calls you will make.
- Modest and unassuming is the most common mindset that I encounter. People think that by saying, 'I can do that' or, 'I am good at that' they will

sound arrogant. This is a total myth when it comes to job applications. If you can't tell an employer what you can do well, he or she will pick someone else who can! So be honest rather than modest and shout out clear and loud what you can do well and be proud of it.

■ Remember that employers aren't mindreaders, so unless you tell them what you can do for them, ideally to make them money or make their life easier, they won't want to take a chance on you.

Now you're ready to conquer the world with a CV or letter for every circumstance, so go out there and be brilliant!

Further reading and weblinks

Books

Creating Winning CVs and Applications, Kathleen Houston, Trotman Publishing
Net that Job! Irene Krechowiecka, Kogan Page
Preparing for Interviews, Julie-Ann Amos, How to Books
Surfing Your Career, Hilary Nickell, How to Books
Your Top 500 CV and Internet Websites, Andrea Watson, Trotman Publishing

Websites

There are many amazing ways to use the Internet for careers information and interesting job vacancies – here are some sites worth checking.

www.prospects.ac.uk is the site for university students and graduates and is an incredible mine of information on careers, with job vacancies advertised as well. It also has excellent advice on job applications, CVs and company selection procedures.

www.monster.co.uk is a fairly typical job site with many interesting features including the Monster Board where your CV can be posted and viewed by employers.

www.nwstudentandgraduate.ac.uk is a specific North-west England site for students and graduates and has excellent job vacancies, employer sectors and good links to other sites. Many university careers services have websites with excellent help and information.

Here is a re-run of my favourite gap year sites:

Study abroad in another country – try **www.aaiuk.org**.

Study in Italy – try **www.arthistoryabroad.com**.

Youth work experience (unpaid) in Africa for four or five months – try **www.aventure.co.uk**.

Conservation experience on game reserves in Africa – try **www.ConservationAfrica.net**.

Young explorers expeditions to Greenland or the Himalayas – try **www.bses.org.uk**.

Summer camp work in America – try **www.bunac.org**.

Sailing, diving, windsurfing training in Greece – try **www.flyingfishonline.com**.

More expeditions – try **www.raleigh.org.uk**.

Voluntary work in this country through your local Council for Voluntary Service, Millennium Volunteers or through Community Service Volunteers – try **www.csv.org.uk**.

Work for a company gaining skills prior to university through the Year In Industry scheme – try **www.yini.org.uk**.

Learn acting techniques and directing and end up at the Edinburgh Festival – try **www.yearoutdrama.com**.

Also check out **www.gapyear.com** and **www.yearoutgroup.org**.